The DAUGHTER Of A SCHIZOPHRENIC MOTHER And A NARCISSISTIC FATHER

A

SH*T

SHOW

BASED ON A
TRUE STORY

By

Susanne Austin

Dedication

I dedicate this book to all members of my family.

Especially my wonderful husband, and my amazing children.

A special thank you for my editor Amber Di Ferdinand

And also Jennifer Givner, my amazing book cover artist.

Preface

Dear Reader,

This is neither a scientific nor psychological book. I am neither a Scientist nor a Doctor. This is a book simply about my observations and my feelings as a child. It is a message that it is not a good idea to clutch the chains that bind you. I am not saying it is easy to let go of those chains. If it was, we would have no need for psychiatrists. There is no easy formula for getting over trauma. Awareness is key! I was asking myself at first: what is awareness, really? I had to think about it. How aware are we of our own thoughts? How aware are we of our feelings? Self-help books are very supportive. The books that helped me the most are Byron Katie's *Loving What Is* as well as Brene Brown's *Daring Greatly*. Jen Sincero's books have also been an inspiration. Their work has surprised me and opened doors for me.

Meditation is a terrific way to connect with the Universe. The Universe is so kind. It will always help us when we ask it. I became a spiritual person just recently. After I have spent decades seeing myself as a victim, I am now at peace with it. I thank my father for the lesson that I do not want to be like him. He has made me kinder and less judgmental. I thank my mother for the hugs and the tenderness in the early years. She has saved me from bitterness. I have so much to be thankful for. I have two healthy children who are grown now, I have the dignity of work, I have a wonderful husband, I enjoy my garden, and continue to find a way to let go of my demons. We are all capable of that. Dear reader, may you always be happy, healthy, and loved! I invite you to join me into the journey of my life. If you have any questions email me at susanne_65@mail.com.

Thank you and good luck in all your endeavors

Chapter 1

The Gentle Heart

"I prize thy gentle heart, free from ambition, falsehood, or art..." (Margaret Fuller)

My mother's name is Margaret. She is the daughter of Ruth and Arnold Berels. Margaret was born in a small German village in 1943. The place had a single convenience store, a church, and a post office. It was a lovely location surrounded by meadows, forests, brooks, and ponds.

Ruth Berels had given birth to Margaret in the big farmhouse that had been in her husband's family for generations. When her midwife had presented her with a daughter, she was vaguely disappointed. It wasn't a tragedy, but she would have preferred a boy. Ruth regretted her thought instantly, and shifted toward gratefulness for a healthy child.

Her husband Arnold was currently a soldier in WW2. His letters from the battle fields were not exactly encouraging. They always said the same thing. Germany cannot win this war. Ruth had always known this. She just wished the end would come soon so everyone could go on with life.

Ruth Berels was a tall, lanky woman. She had high cheekbones and a rather plain face. While no one would have called her beautiful, she made up for it in spades with sharp intelligence. She had a strong personality, made good quick decisions, and was not afraid to give her opinion even when it was controversial.

She was born into a culture where the husband is head of the household. I am sure that she secretly had issues with this concept, considering the fact that she was highly intelligent. But she was also a product of her upbringing. She was a strict Catholic and did not question the beliefs of that faith. As a child, Ruth had openly dared to contradict one of the basic Catholic rules. It had not sat well with her when she was assigned babysitting duties by her mother. She described the following example to me once. She had been forced to watch her younger siblings most of the afternoons of the week. As always, she had resented this chore. She would have much rather worked in the fields instead. She had grudgingly accepted her mother's order though. She remembered the

Bible and the fourth commandment: honor thy father and thy mother. On this day, however, her temper was too close to the surface. She addressed her mother in a calm voice which belied her fury.

"Mama, why do we have so many children anyway? I am sick and tired being forced to take care of them all the time."

That earned her a slap for her impertinence. Even though it wasn't a hard blow, it emphasized the point that she had gone too far. All in all though, my grandmother assured me she had a wonderful childhood. She had been born into a middle class family that provided plenty of good food, a roof over her head, and money enough for fun.

Ruth married at the age of twenty-three. A farmer she had met in a nearby village had asked for her hand in marriage and her father gave permission. I have always secretly wondered why my grandmother had married a man like Arnold Berels. He was taciturn and often had a grouchy disposition.

One day I asked her without preamble, "Grandma why did you marry my grandpa?"

Her answer was instant, "I wanted to be a farmer's wife."

That did not satisfy me so I probed further. "Did you love him?"

She hesitated, "Love is a strong word. I liked him, would be more accurate. He had a farm, and I have always wanted one, so when he proposed I said yes. Don't be so shocked child. Even in today's world, marriages are often a practical thing."

While Arnold Berels had an aloof personality, he was also hardworking and not overly bright. He was good looking though, with his black hair and dark eyes. He was of medium height, slightly below Ruth's 5 feet 8. When Ruth came into his life, he was delighted. Her practicality, common sense, intelligence, and her matter of fact attitude appealed to him. Of course, no matter how smart she was, she was still in a class below him. Women just were; that was a given. The Bible said so and it has always been that way. Still it could not hurt to have a decent brain in the family. He would allow her to make some family decisions because he recognized her brain power as an asset.

After her marriage, Ruth had to work the farm by herself. Her husband got almost instantly drafted as a soldier in WW2. Shouldering the work and new motherhood was not easy for Ruth. There was not much time to bond with baby Margaret. Ruth ran the farm and left the care of the baby to a kind neighbor woman. With the help of the village community, Ruth worked the fields, tended the life stock, kept the house clean, cooked, butchered, worked the vegetable garden, and many other chores.

In the war days, it was not unusual for beggars to come to Ruth's door. She always gave them some food, but she did not exactly feel safe without a man in the house. She seriously contemplated getting a dog to feel more secure. Her cousin Irma owned a German Shepard and that dog had puppies a year ago. Ruth decided she would walk the three miles to Irma's house and take one of the puppies off her hands.

Margaret was a year old now and was absolutely delighted when Ruth brought the dog home. They named him Wolf. He was mostly tied up in the hallway, announcing any stranger who entered the house. It was not a great life for the dog, to be tied up all day and his only distraction was the toddler Margaret. She paid attention to him, played with him, and petted him. The dog thanked her by loving her. Margaret reciprocated that sentiment.

She was an obedient child who did not give Ruth too much trouble. By the age of three, she did her chores willingly and eagerly. She fed the chickens, helped with the weeds in the vegetable garden, and did simple cleaning chores around the house. Gradually her chores increased. Margaret was fascinated with her mother at a very early age. Ruth was an impressive figure, a working machine who never complained and never cried. Margaret's admiration for her mother warred with the lack of compassion and tenderness that Ruth also emanated. This void of maternal love would create a scarcity in Margaret's life that would haunt her.

It was the year 1948 when Arnold Barrels returned to his wife and his daughter. He had been captured in France and was finally released. Ruth was relieved and nervous at the same time. She could use the help and share the responsibility. However, she had to admit that it would take some adjustment. She had gotten used to being in charge.

Life went on and the family settled into a routine. Margaret got used to her father and secretly thought he was just as distant and austere as her mother was. As Margaret grew older, her playtime became more and more restricted. She was used as a field hand when harvest and planting time came. That meant those golden summers of childhood were limited to her. While the rest of the village children her age enjoyed the carefree time of summer vacation filled with playtime and socializing, Margaret worked in the fields all day. She was experiencing loneliness very early in her life. Most adults have a hard time dealing with the feeling of isolation. How hard must it be for a child who was already aware of her parent's lack of affection. This was not the only trouble Margaret faced. She had problems expressing herself. She could not put into words what she felt. It did not help that her parents were so inapproachable. These circumstances left her lonely before she had even learned the art of socializing.

These were the first deep cracks in Margaret's soul. She was deprived of developing her own personality. She had no time to play or make real friends. I do not think either of her parents were aware of this. Her mother was too busy with chores and her father never bothered to analyze what was on anyone's mind, let alone on what was in his child's head.

When Margaret was six years old, she became an older sister. She was overjoyed. Ruth's second child was a boy. They named him Gerald. Margaret delighted in taking care of her baby brother. She could lavish all her pent-up tenderness on the baby. No doubt she harbored the hope that she would be released from the field work, in order to take care of her baby brother. Her hopes were dashed almost instantly. Ruth immediately went into negotiations with her neighbor to take over the care of baby Gerald. This meant no break from the field work for Margaret.

When Margaret was eight years old, a traumatic event happened in her life. The incident was intense enough to haunt her into adulthood. It was fall and the harvest was already in, and Margaret had the luxury of fun and games at last. Whenever she went on a playdate with one of her friends, she untied Wolf and took him with her. The dog was grateful and he and Margaret formed a deep relationship with one another. There is something special about animals in a depressed person's life. They are always happy to see you, they do not judge you, and they give you unrestrained tenderness. Wolf balanced out some of the voids in Margaret's life.

On this particular day, her father had a visitor. He had come to discuss business with him. Arnold needed more grazing lands for his cattle and they were discussing a deal. Ruth served refreshments and Margaret was playing quietly in her room. Wolf was tied up in the hallway as always. He had not liked the visitor and had growled at him when he passed by. After the business between Arnold and the visitor was concluded, he was ready to leave. He passed the hallway again and this time Wolf did more than growl; he bit the man in his leg. The fellow yelped and cursed at his torn pants. He did not take the deal back, but did not leave on amicable terms either.

Arnold was enraged at the dog. He untied him and led him down to the stables. Then he grabbed his rifle and shot Wolf. Margaret had heard the commotion involving the dog, the visitor, and her father's cursing. When she heard the gun shot, she felt her own heart exploding with grief. She knew instantly what had happened. The heartache was so intense that she felt the sadness choking her soul. Her tears seemed unending. Her faithful friend was gone at the hands of her father. The sweetest part of her existence was no longer present in her life, his life cut short, only because he had done his duty and protected the house. The pressure on her heart was so massive that her whole body ached. Her soul already had deep cracks in it from lack of nurturing and this event added another deep cut at her very core. She was only a child, but she knew very little of what a childhood should be. While time usually heals most wounds, there are some cracks that will mark the soul forever.

Margaret's fragile bond with her father seemed even more brittle now. Her frail self-confidence was now shaken even further. She began blaming herself for Wolf's death. She should have done something to save him. She blamed her father for regarding life so cheap, she blamed her mother for not stopping her husband, and most off all she blamed herself for not interfering. The judge inside of her was the harshest tyrant of all. Had she blocked her father's way when he took Wolf to the stable? No, she hadn't, she had cried and let it happen. And now her Wolf was dead and she would never again take him on walks. The deep pain produced fresh tears. She had learned that animals could not go to heaven, but she prayed that God would make an exception in Wolf's case.

I asked my grandmother about the incident with Wolf decades later. She did not even recall it. How lonely my poor mother must have been when her own mother was not even aware of the terrible hurt inside of her. I voiced as much to my grandmother. She looked at me thoughtfully.

"Child, life was different in those days. Everything was about work. This was reconstruction time in Germany. We had lost the war and were determined to rebuild our country. That was the most dominant thought on our minds. There was just no time to cuddle with our children, and even communication with them was very limited. You must also understand that the times were different then. These days, children are regarded as precious. In those days, there was still the rule that children should be heard but not seen. That did not mean that we did not love our kids, but society did not fully recognize them until they reached a certain age."

Margaret was twelve years old when Ruth gave birth to her third and final child. It was another boy. They named him Arnold after his father. Margaret was delighted as being the big sister of another baby brother. At twelve years old, her features suggested great beauty. She had high cheekbones, jet black curly hair, and deep brown eyes. Her rosy, healthy complexion rounded out her good looks. Despite her striking physical appearance, Margaret seemed free of vanity.

Ruth recalled a conversation she had with one of Margaret's teacher once. There were discussing Margaret's school performances. He said that she was an average student who had trouble with mathematics. He also mentioned the girl's introverted disposition. Then he expressed some worry about Margaret. He said her exceptional good looks would likely attract a wrong husband. Ruth had never forgotten this conversation. It left her with an ominous feeling, that she found hard to shake.

The discussion with Margaret's teacher had also given Ruth food for thought. She did worry about her daughter. The girl was too serious and too religious. Ruth herself was a Catholic through and through, but she worried that her daughter's faith bordered on the fanatic. Her constant praying was beyond what Ruth deemed normal. She found her kneeling in her room at any time of the day, she heard her murmuring prayers while doing her field work constantly, and she saw her going to church daily. The holy mother Mary in particular, was Margaret's fantasy of a merciful substitute mother figure.

Shortly after Margaret's fourteenth birthday, Ruth found out exactly what was in her daughter's heart. It was late afternoon and Ruth and Margaret were preparing dinner. They had just about finished their preparations when Margaret announced that she wanted to talk to her mother. Ruth interrupted her work for once, poured them both a cup of coffee, and sat down expectantly at the dining room table. Margaret seemed nervous and said nothing for a moment, just looking at her mother's face intently. Then she took a deep breath and went straight to the heart of the matter.

"Mama, I want to become a nun," she announced.

Ruth looked at her daughter in astonishment. Whatever she had been expecting, this was not it. She stayed silent for a moment and tried to digest the news. A nun, she thought. She was surprised that she did not like the sound of it. It was bewildering to her. She was a devout Catholic. So, why wasn't she happy that her daughter wanted to devote her life to God? She was not sure about the answer. She would have to think about this one, long and hard.

To buy time, she asked with uncharacteristic gentleness, "Why do you want to become a nun, my child?"

Margaret's answer came swift and without hesitation. The words came bubbling out in a rush, "Mama I want to live in a convent. I want to serve God; I want to adore the holy mother Mary. I want to go to mass and do prayers in the morning. I want to work in the gardens, do cleaning chores, and have kitchen duties, while living in a peaceful and serene environment. Such a workday would make me very happy. I am sure I would be very content in a convent."

Ruth listened with apt attention. She had to admit that she understood her daughter quite well. She considered the matter in her head. Margaret was a dutiful and obedient daughter. Those qualities would come in handy in a convent. She was submissive by nature, which was perfect for a nun. She would love it. It suited her heart. She would be fully engaged and connected and that, Ruth recognized would soothe Margaret's soul. The knowledge that becoming a nun would make Margaret happy, did not sit well with Ruth however. She was not sure exactly as to the why. Why didn't she want Margaret to become a nun? Ruth did what she seldom tried. She examined her heart. Maybe deep down, she did not want to lose her daughter. As a nun Margaret would not give her grandchildren. She would not be able to talk to her on a regular basis. When it came right down to it, Ruth did not want to be deprived of her daughter's company. Selfish? Maybe, but it was the truth. It occurred to Ruth that she loved her daughter more than she realized. It was a rare admission indeed, for Ruth to have such feelings. She was not quite sure how to deal with that. She would figure it out in time, that was certain.

In any case Margaret was only fourteen years old. She would have to be at least eighteen before a transfer to a convent could become reality. Plenty of time to change her mind. At that moment Ruth knew that if at age eighteen Margaret still wanted to go to a convent, she would give her blessing. She had earned it. While Ruth was deep into her own thoughts, Margaret watched her mother carefully over her coffee cup. She waited with baited breath for an answer.

Then Ruth shocked her by taking Margaret's hand into hers. Nothing could have surprised Margaret more. Ruth had never done this before. She looked deep into her daughter's eyes and finally answered.

"Margaret, let me begin by saying you are a good daughter. You have never given me any grief and your happiness means a lot to me. As for you going to a convent, if that remains your wish, I will not stand in your way. Furthermore, I would clear the way with your father as well. As it stands right now, you will have to wait four more years until you are eighteen. If after all this time you still want to join a convent, you will have my blessing for your enterprise."

Margaret's eyes filled with unexpected tears. This had been a very unusual talk with her mother. Ruth may have lacked hugs and kisses, but her words had been tender just this once. The deep admiration Margaret had always had for her mother was intensified. She had always loved Ruth, but at this moment her heart warmed. She would always treasure this particular heart to heart talk with her mother.

In the time that followed, Ruth watched Margaret more carefully than before. Both tried to improve communication with one another. This was neither easy, nor was it very successful, but making the effort was good for both mother and daughter.

Meanwhile, Margaret had become a beautiful girl. She was overwhelmed with young men who wanted to date her.

She declined all offers gently, which did not discourage the young men. Her sweetness made her even more attractive. She was in many ways irresistible to men. Beauty and generosity of spirit was such a rare combination.

Margaret was not a very social person by nature. She craved nothing more than peace and quiet. She was also very modest in a natural way. In a convent, she would have found exactly what she had wanted all her life. She would have daydreamed and prayed and worshipped her life away, and would have been happy and fulfilled.

I wonder, and this is only speculation on my part, if she would have ever developed full-fledged schizophrenia if she had gone to a convent. Somehow, I think she would have not, at least not as severe.

Life was mostly uneventful for the next couple of years for Margaret. She had settled her thoughts into joining a convent and was preparing herself mentally for that future. She seldom went out with her girlfriends and virtually never went on dates.

A week before her eighteenth birthday Margaret's friend Irmgard coaxed Margaret out of her reverie. She persuaded her to join her at the annual village carnival. It would be this event that would give Margaret's life a different turn and would alter her dreams forever.

Chapter 2

The Mind of an Egotist

"Selfishness is not living as one wishes to live, it is asking others to live as one wishes to live" (Oscar Wilde)

Bernhard

My father's name is Bernhard Dreier. He was born in 1937, two years before the outbreak of World War 2. I researched his family background as best as I could, but in many ways it remains sketchy. I knew my grandparents on my father's side fairly well, since they lived in the same house I grew up in. They lived in their own separate unit one floor above us.

My grandmother had a toxic personality. She loved gossip above everything. Putting people down was her main pleasure in life. She was very righteous and thought of herself as superior in every way. She lacked a sense of humor and may well have been a narcissist herself.

I have contradicting accounts of my grandfather. My own as his granddaughter were very favorable. He bought me candy, chocolate, and toys. He was kind and unlike my grandmother, he had a sense of humor. There were other opinions about him from various relatives. It was rumored that he had affairs and was abusive when he was drunk. I had trouble believing this as a child because I had never seen that behavior from him. Then again, I had not known him until he was already at an advanced age. Later when my father used domestic violence on my mother, her mother-in-law watched with satisfaction. Her exact words to my mother were: "Why should you have it any better than I did?"

Jealousy is a strange thing. There is a saying and I think it is true: Jealously merely measures lover's insecurity. I think my grandmother was jealous of her husband in various ways. I am not sure if he had affairs, but if he did, it was unlikely he could have kept them secret in such a small town. My grandmother would have certainly found out. She would have kept silent, for she was a proud woman. It would have eaten her up inside though. She resented her husband's freedom, or the freedom of men in general. In those days, men finished their work days and then it was time for their pleasures. Wives were excluded from those pleasant distractions. They joined a bowling club, played cards or dice in pubs, or were socializing with their coworkers.

Meanwhile their wives hung out the clothes, tended to their children, sewed, and were tied up in their houses. They had nothing but gossip and monotony. Their almighty husbands saw them as their personal property. Aside from house cleaning and rearing children, it was their job to keep their husbands happy. I don't think this sat well with some of them, especially my grandmother. I did feel her bitterness about her restricted life. Talking maliciously about other people was her only salvation.

One must consider the times as well. My father was a child during World War 2 and was still one in the aftermath of the war. He faced food shortages, heard bombs crashing into buildings, and saw people in a panic taking shelter in basements. Aside from that, he also lacked his father during that time, since he was a soldier in the war. These must have been traumatic times for a little boy. The lethal disposition of his mother during these tough times did not make it any easier.

His mother was hard to please. She was a tough woman who lacked compassion and empathy. She liked to find fault in the slightest mistakes and her drive to perfectionism was almost obsessive. While she held herself to that impossible standard, she expected her children to do likewise. The slightest misstep was met with extreme rage. She made sure that her children were the best behaved, smartest, and prettiest kids in town. God forbid they put her to shame in anyway. Their manners had to be perfect, as did their dress code. She wanted the title of being the best mother in town. It never entered her head that her children had to pay the price for her mania.

I do believe that law of perfection in his childhood shaped my father throughout his life. I do wonder, and not for the first time, if he had a secret hatred for all females. He may not have even been aware of that hate. Without a doubt though, he thought females were his property. His mother was the only female he respected (and I do believe deep down resented her all his life at the same time). He always claimed he loved his mother more than anyone, but narcissism does not allow for love. The unfortunate condition of narcissism prevents the sufferer from obtaining real love.

I am not a psychiatrist, but my observation with narcissists is an extremely obstinate behavior. They are so inflexible. They think that they are infallible. They are always right and they are always perfect. They do not make mistakes. It is unthinkable that they could be wrong. They are the dictator of their families. Leniency is a word, that a narcissist does not understand.

Whatever the case, I have learned in the course of my life that it is possible to learn tolerance and that it is a valuable concept. I have learned that it is often better to be kind than right. This last phenomenon came to me recently and it still needs a lot of practice. I am also learning to change ingrained behavior inside of me and I can say with confidence that it is possible.

Back to Bernhard! He was the oldest of four children. Two sisters and a brother. As the oldest he naturally felt superior to his siblings. This sentiment was strengthened by the encouragement of his mother. She put him in charge of his brother and his sister. This hierarchy suited my father just fine. My father was a physically attractive child and his mother basked in the attention he would get for his good looks. This attention to his striking appeal must have made a lasting impression on the young Bernhard. In a way it must have fed his insecurities right from the start. He had his mother's worship and her harshest criticism. This emotional roller coaster is tough for a child. It promotes fear and shame. A lethal combination even for an adult to live with, but for a child in their formative years really hard to overcome.

I wonder what my father would have done had he found out that his brother was gay. I do not think he knew this fact in his youth, but I could be wrong about that. His brother, Karl, was the so-called black sheep of the family. I remember him as a humorous and good-natured man. I have never suspected him to be gay until I found out in my late teens. I wonder now, if his family had somehow found out about his sexual orientation, and how lost he must have felt. The shame and isolation they would have put on him would have been beyond cruel. An admission to homosexuality would have had catastrophic consequences for him. No way would he have been allowed to be himself. I did sense a hidden sadness in him. It was in sharp contrast with his fun-loving personality. To this day, some people think that homosexuality is a shameful thing.

Now I ask myself, for what? Why put a man through that ordeal of loneliness and pain? Only because he is gay? So, what if he was? For fear of neighbor's gossip? What do those opinions really matter in a short life? And who are we, to dictate a man's sexual orientation? Are we saying, if you are gay, you have no right of a sex life? How arrogant is that? If only we weren't so intolerant of one another. Yes, me included. I was not always flexible either. Why is it so hard to accept people as they are? I think the answer is simple. We all lack broad-mindedness and awareness. If only we had an alarm in our head that would say: Stop! You are afflicting fear, pain and shame on another person! Maybe the world would be a better place. I am working on installing such alarm bells into my own head. I am not always successful but I know, if I find a way for more tolerance for others, I will be a happier person.

My father was a narcissist and his upbringing fueled his condition. As I said before, if I had known that he suffered from an illness, my life would have been somewhat easier. As it was, I did not know that as a child and I did not understand it either. This not understanding made it even harder for me. I harbored a longstanding hatred for my father growing up. That cost me a lot of energy and pain and wasted a great deal of my time and happiness.

Let's take a look at what narcissism really is. There is an explanation in the German dictionary that the word comes from "Narzissmus" and means the never-ending agony of the partner. The website activebeat.com by Katherine George put it this way: "Narcissism comes from the Greek word Narcissus, a man who sees his own reflection in a pool of water and falls in love with it." While an exaggerated sense of one's own attractiveness is certainly one of the characteristics of Narcissistic Personality Disorder (NPD), there are many other symptoms that indicate someone suffering from this mental condition.

The same website from Katherine George continues:

"Narcissists do always talk about themselves. They always talk about their appearance, their talents, their achievements. They lack empathy. They do not understand other people's feelings or needs. For example, you say that a person has cancer and they talk about their new car. Narcissists have little regard for people around them, this is especially true for the feelings of their partners. They also fantasize, and their dreams revolve around success, power, beauty or the perfect spouse. As a result of such imaginings, they feel they should have the best of everything, including houses cars, clothing, or other status affirming things, such as the best medical care and schooling. Unfortunately, these fantasies are a way for narcissists to fend off inner emptiness, feeling special and in control and avoid feelings of ineffectiveness and insignificance. And because they are rarely rooted in reality, it can lead to immense frustration and anger if these visions are not achieved…"

Katherine George goes on. The following is a list of some more of her findings:

1. They also believe they are superior to everyone. They have a grandiose sense of self-importance leading them to feel superior to just about anyone. They believe that others, who are just as special as they are, are the only ones who can truly understand them. In order to remain feelings of superiority, they will resort to belittling others by focusing on their flaws whether they are real or imagined. For narcissists, this is an effective way to hide their own shortcomings and preserve their self- image.

2. In addition to that, they require constant praise, she states. Despite appearing outwardly confident, they are often incredibly insecure and have a very fragile self-esteem. In order to keep themselves propped up, they require constant praise and admiration. They also need to be recognized as superior even without achievements to warrant it.

3. This fragility when it comes to their sense of their own self also makes a narcissist highly reactive to criticism. Any comment that shines a spotlight on their insecurities or flaws may be met with a burst of rage, causing a person to lie or divert the conversation into an entirely different direction.

4. Next is their sense of entitlement. People with NPD have a sense of self entitlement, expecting others to offer them special favors and fulfill their requests without questions. If such a treatment isn't awarded to them, they may become impatient or angry. Narcissists view others as existing primarily for their own needs. This behavior is not unlike a toddler who has never learned he is not the center of attention in the world and becomes enraged when others don't meet his immediate needs and demands. This is the end of Katherine George's assessment. I found even more useful research done by Mrs. George.

Narcissists also definitely take advantage of others. According to WebMD, people are naturally drawn to narcissists finding them attractive, charismatic, and exciting. It only becomes complicated when the narcissists needs are not met. Narcissists often have very tumultuous friendships and romantic relationships are short lived. Here is a list of what the WebMD page, also by Katherine George, found on narcissism.

1. They have a huge envy of others. Because of their low self-esteem and need to be superior, narcissists see people who have things they don't, such as tangible things, status, or admiration, as threats. Interestingly, narcissists also believe that people are envious of them. And while this is exactly the type of attention a narcissist wants, accusing people of such feelings may put an immediate end to the friendship.

2. Narcissists like to dominate conversations; they have a hard time listening and feel compelled to talk about

themselves and exaggerate their accomplishments. Another typical trait of narcissism is a lack of empathy. They have an inability or unwillingness to recognize the needs of feeling of others. Often times a person with NPD seems totally unreasonable and outrageously insensitive.

3. Boundless ambition is another characteristic of narcissism. They fantasize of being the best of the best. They constantly visualize how powerful they will be, how much more beautiful they are compared to anyone else, and how much richer. Their sense of entitlement and superiority is why they tend to only associate themselves with high status people and obsess over status symbols.

4. It does not make sense with all these characteristics, but narcissists are incredibly insecure, and need to put down other people to feed their fragile self-esteem. The insecurity of a fragile narcissist, often seems to stem from the fact that they internally question themselves whether or not they are truly special and unique and therefore are more likely to seek and rely on positive affirmation from others. Vulnerable narcissists need to put down people and impose their power on them.

5. Often narcissists are incredibly charming at first glance. As relationships progress, their behavior becomes demeaning and aggressive. Their seeming confidence and charm are smoke screens.

6. Next, we take a look at a narcissist's extreme competitiveness. Narcissists strive to win whatever it takes.

There is no in between winning or losing for them. They have to win since they are always better than anyone else in their mind. Their incessant need to win contributes to their inability to celebrate other people's successes, even or especially their own family members. They can never put themselves in a vulnerable position where they do not feel superior to their opponent. And they hold grudges forever.

7. On the outside narcissists might seem they are extremely confident and they don't care what other people think, but they are extremely vulnerable of other people's opinions, more than anyone else in fact. They care deeply about maintain a perfect image of themselves. As a result, they do not take kindly to any sort of insult whether imagined or real. They take criticism as a personal attack and a huge insult. They also feel slighted and abandoned and they don't get over it. Their inability to handle faults in themselves and others go much deeper than is natural. They are unable to cope when things don't go their way and will never admit to fault of their own.

8. Narcissists are extremely aggressive when their own failures get detected. When confronted with a weakness even in a neutral way they can react with sudden and surprisingly harsh outbursts of yelling, crying, anger, or other aggressive behaviors. At this point, I like to thank Katherine George for her accurate description of narcissism.

My father displayed all these narcissistic behaviors to the fullest. He was a narcissist to a T. Of course, I did not understand this condition as a child and I barely understand it now. My father must have been in constant torture, for he was in no way special, at least not in the way that his condition demanded. He must have been hard pressed to meet his own standards, because he had a low paying job and was not overly bright. He saw himself as perfect, but only when he pointed out how imperfect the members of his family were, his neighbors, and his friends. However, most of his neighbors were better off than he was and that must have irked him considerably. As a result, he was dissatisfied and it fueled an enormous aggression in him. He constantly had to find a way to put people down, or he would have been eaten up by envy.

I recognize now that there must have been a terrible pressure inside of him because he was so far beneath of what he thought he should have. This scarcity made him brutal and cruel. He had to put everyone in the universe down to combat the deep emptiness in him. Since he was extremely unhappy, he could not stand to see anyone happy. So, he found ways to fill his inside desolation by putting people down. And since his own family was closest, and the most vulnerable, they were targeted first and foremost. They were his easiest target after all.

I think when he was a child the first people he put down were his siblings. They were all younger than him and easily overpowered. My uncle Karl drank himself to death when he was not even fifty years old. Had my father found out his secret of homosexuality and tortured him about it? Or could he not live with the supposed shame he had put on his family? I guess I will never know. Alcoholism was definitely present in my father's family. His father was a heavy drinker, my uncle died from it, and my father drank a lot as well.

When my father met my mother, the disastrous relationship between a schizophrenic and a narcissist began, and lasted for over fifty years.

Chapter 3

Schizophrenia and Narcissism

Welcome to the Shit Show

We checked out my father's condition, now let's take a look at my mother's disorder. Etavocaycenter.org states the following: "The exact cause of schizophrenia is unknown. Many researchers believe several factors can contribute including biochemical, genetic and environmental. Multiple studies also show that individuals with serious mental illnesses are especially vulnerable of being victimized. This frequency involves theft, or money but also indicates violent victimization such as psychical and sexual assault emotional abuse and being killed. Women who have a severe psychiatric disease, are especially vulnerable."

Mary V. Seeman says, "Schizophrenia has been a severe and persistent illness, that disqualifies mother's from adequately parenting their children. To understand the scope of that issue let's take a look at it. About half the women diagnosed with schizophrenia are mothers. The rate of custody loss in this group is high. Most women with schizophrenia value their role as mothers and their adult children remain attached to them. Most of their problems appear to be not in the illness itself, but by associated risks of poverty substance abuse, domestic violence and social isolation."

A child of a mother diagnosed with paranoid schizophrenia experiences a lack of attachment with their mother during childhood. It is reflected in difficulties with intimacy and trust in their adult relationships, which causes depression. From my observation schizophrenics can also be manipulative. My mother could be extremely stubborn and used some of her illness for manipulation. I will go into more detail on this matter as the story unfolds.

Before going on with my tale, I would like to explain something about schizophrenia and sexuality. Despite a healthy interest in sex, many people with schizophrenia report a digressive deterioration of their sexual and socio-sexual functioning beginning in young adulthood, closely paralleling the age of onset of their illness. For example, estrogen, a key hormone for sexual functioning, is lower than normal in females with schizophrenia at the onset of illness. Similarly, lower levels of gonadotropins and testosterone have been observed in unmedicated males with the disorder. Together these findings suggest that these hormonal disturbances contribute to the sexual dysfunction associated with the disorder.

Sexual dysfunctions may also result directly or indirectly from symptoms of the disorder and their functional consequences. For example, individuals with schizophrenia have low self-confidence, few personal relationships, loss of impulse control, and negative or deficit symptoms, such as lack of interest and loss of pleasure, all of which may result in sexual problems. Given their social anxiety and deficits in social perception, sexual dysfunction can be a source of demoralization and discouragement in seeking sex with appropriate partners. In addition to that, the medicine and antidepressant medications commonly prescribed may actually contribute to the sexual dysfunction in schizophrenics.

I am not a psychiatrist nor a researcher and can only speak from what I have observed in the course of the first twenty years of my life. I did know that my parents had sexual problems. It was in part due to my mother's condition, but only in part. My father did his share to cause problems in that department as well. I will get to that later in this book.

To understand this relationship of my parents, one must be a genius. God knows to this day I do not fully understand what was going on. But having done the research, a few things did become clear to me. My mother, overworked as a child, wanted a peaceful marriage raising children, being a housewife, tending the garden, and pour to all her love on husband and kids. That was her expectation and her dream. My father wanted control first and foremost. He wanted a family so he could have a people under his direct power. He was highly dissatisfied with his life already and needed a family to feed his ego. He had wanted to travel, but was never able to come up with the necessary money to make that dream come true. So, ruling over a family was the next best thing. Both of them would find out that their expectations were pipe dreams that were very far from the reality they would experience. This union was a disaster, not only for them, but for their children as well. Knowing what I know now, this relationship could not work.

A narcissist with his need for perfection and control is just a very bad fit for a schizophrenic. I can see why my father thought that my mother was the best fit for him. He thought of her as very weak and easily manipulated. In his mind, those were exactly the qualities that he sought in a woman. He did not know that my mother was schizophrenic and my mother did not know it at the time either. I have now done my research on the condition and have to smile at this point. A schizophrenic element in a marriage is a real wild card. I think it is fair to say that my mother actually learned a few things in the art of manipulation from her "loving" husband.

My mother also had the faulty notion that her love would change my father. As I mentioned earlier, she was a fanatic Catholic and was convinced that prayer and tenderness could change anyone. She was wrong about that and her marriage would prove that.

Upon interviewing my mother in my later years, I asked her why on earth they had wanted children. Or had my brother and I been an accident? My mother was quite surprised by the question.

She said, "Of course I wanted children and your father wanted them even more than me. In the first week, when we just got married, he asked me daily if I was pregnant."

This statement stunned me. Narcissists, I would imagine, would not want children. Children were a lot of work. They needed nurture and patience. Why would he want that kind of commitment? I had to check this out and hit the internet. Here is what I found on that subject.

"Narcissists parents will never understand the breadth of their impact on kids," says Seth Meyers PsyD. He then continues, "The topic of narcissism begs the following question flashing in neon lights: Why would a narcissist want a child to begin with? Aren't they so focused on themselves that they wouldn't have the slightest interest in paying attention to others, much less attending a needy young child who craves constant attention and praise?"

Seth Meyers then answers his own questions. "Alas the question presumes a type of normalcy and natural order of the parent child relationship that betrays the root of narcissism. The truth is, narcissistic parents don't have children because they want to nurture and guide their offspring through life, they have children so they have an automatic, built in relationship in which they have all the power, one in which the narcissist can write the rules without any checks and balances. Understand this: Control over something else is the ultimate jackpot every narcissist work so hard to win. The reality of narcissistic parenting couldn't be sadder. The child of the narcissist realizes early on that he exists to serve the parent- not the other way around. And that is only the beginning of Dr. Meyers findings. The list goes on:

1. Narcissists mess up the life of a child without suffering any consequences themselves. The real tragedy occurs behind closed doors at home, much like the process of psychical abuse, Meyers went on. The problem with being the child of a narcissist is that it takes these children so many years of frustration and anguish to figure out that mom or dad isn't quite right, until that point, these children are merely dancing as fast as they can, trying to please the impossible to please the narcissistic parent. It takes years to finally see that type of parenting they've been receiving is wrong-if not emotionally abusive.

2. Young children of narcissists learn early in life that everything they do is a reflection on the parent, to the point that the child must fit into the personality and behavior mold intended for them. These children bear tremendous anxiety from a young age as they must continually push aside their own personality in order to please the parent and provide the mirror image that the parent so desperately needs. If these children fail to comply with the narcissists wishes or try to set their own goals for their life- God forbid- the children will be overly punished frozen out, or avoided for a period of time, or how it was in my case sexually abused.

3. Furthermore, Meyers states, with young children the narcissistic parent is as experienced as unpredictable and confusing. Narcissists are extremely difficult for adults to understand, let alone children. Because young children cannot make sense of the narcissist tricks, these children internalize intense shame. (I keep failing mom, I am so stupid, something is wrong with me). The overall bond between a narcissistic parent and a child is weak. Deep down the child does not feel constantly loved, and the child recognizes the narcissistic program: You are only as good as I say you are, and you will be loved only if you comply with my wishes. Simply put, it's truly heartbreaking for the child.

I was born in such an alliance. My mother got pregnant immediately after she got married. My father was ecstatic. Not because he wanted to nurture a child, but as mentioned above, to integrate it into his court and serve his needs. I am sure this thought did not even occur to my mother and how could it? She was not aware at the time and maybe not even now, that he had a mental condition.

Chapter 4

Margaret and Bernhard

A Disastrous Combination

"Politics doesn't make strange bedfellows - marriage does"
(Groucho Marx)

Margaret was attending a social function at last. She had resisted it for so long and now her friend Irmgard had succeeded in persuading her to show up at the annual village festival. Maybe it was just as well, she thought, this would be her last public event for a while, maybe even forever. She would soon become a nun, and then she had all the time in the world for solitude and prayer. The sacrifice of missing out on fairs was not particularly painful to her. In her heart she knew she could easily live without them.

Upon arriving at the fairgrounds, Margaret thought, it is pleasant to be here after all. She saw the twinkling lights of the roller coasters, she smelled the funnel cakes, bratwurst, hot dogs, and the beer. She heard the waltz music from the carousel and the latest hits from the bumper cars.

The two girls were immediately spotted by a group of friends. Heads turned when it was clear that Irmgard was actually accompanied by Margaret. She was a rare appearance to be sure. She was, without even being aware of it, the center of attention. Personally, she did not care much for the role either. Not that she thought of herself as a wallflower, but in her mind, she was neither a sophisticated flirt nor glamorous. It never occurred to her that the lack of those qualities made her unique and different and therefore highly desirable. Of course, her outward appearance easily caught the eye of men. She had a natural beauty, young and fresh, and a sweetness that appealed to every male's pride.

Everyone who knew Margaret was aware of the fact that she had never had a boyfriend. She had plenty of offers but so far had refused them all. There was an enigma about Margaret Berels that every full-blooded male in close proximity wanted to crack. So far, none of them had been able to solve the riddle.

Margaret was surrounded by friends, but she felt strangely detached. Her thoughts were occupied with becoming a nun. She did not really need this kind of entertainment. It was pleasant to be here but not important.

In a nearby tent, Bernhard was sitting on a long table, a girl on his lap, drinking a glass of beer and smoking a cigarette. He was boasting to his friends about his latest soccer prowess. In his last game he had single handedly carried his team to victory. While bragging in a loud voice, one hand on his beer glass and the other sliding up Heidi's knee, Bernhard was in his full element. He was the center of attention, every girl's dream, able to hold his liquor, and the king of the table. He was charming and had a sense of humor and was better than everybody and that's the way he liked it. Yes, this was life at its best.

It was at that moment that Margaret and Irmgard entered the beer tent. They were carrying plates with funnel cakes and were looking for a table. This was not easy, because the tent was crowded with people.

Bernhard saw them entering and for a moment he was stunned. He had never seen Margaret before, but he spotted her beauty immediately. The girl was an amazing looker, he thought. He also noticed the hungry stares of the other males in the room. She would be his, he thought, there was no doubt about it. His predatory instincts went into overdrive. All the men in the room waved at the two girls, and beckoned them to join their table.

Bernhard threw Heidi unceremoniously to the side, ignored her hurt look, and marched up to the two young ladies. He positioned himself between them, laid an arm around their waists, and guided them to his table. He was aware and delighted that many of the men in this tent were secretly wishing him to hell for his quick move and he openly reveled in the knowledge.

Once seated at the table, Bernhard took over the conversation and entertained them with tales from his life. Irmgard had seen Bernhard before but had never had a conversation with him. He was always surrounded by pretty girls and he had the reputation of a being a ladies' man. He could always have his pick. She also knew that she was sitting at this table only by Margaret's grace. As always when Margaret chose to attend an event, she attracted men like a magnet. It was most infuriating that she never even tried, thought Irmgard enviously. She looked at Bernard with yearning eyes, but his attention was glued on Margaret.

It surprised Irmgard that Margaret seemed to be taken by this man for once. She was still on her guard but her impenetrable walls seemed to crumble a bit. She was laughing at his jokes and seemed to have the time of her life. Irmgard had never seen her like that. Margaret looked amazing at any time, but right at this moment, she seemed more radiant than ever. Bernhard asked Margaret to dance and as they walked to the dance floor, Irmgard watched with interest how Margaret would handle this man when he had her in his arms.

It made Irmgard smile. Bernhard, feeling secure of his presence with women, held Margaret tight. Her smile widened significantly seeing Margaret's struggle to keep him at arms lengths. This, she imagined, would certainly be something new for Bernhard. He was used to girls trying to seduce him, and he always was all too willing to comply. With Margaret it would be different. This was perhaps the first girl he had ever met who was holding him at a distance. Irmgard knew Margaret well enough to know that she was not playing hard to get, but that she was just being herself.

Suddenly Irmgard felt a strange trepidation. She hoped Margaret would not get hurt by this man. She was so innocent, so sweet and inexperienced. If she fell for Bernhard, she would be heartbroken. And then Irmgard put her fears aside. Bernhard would lose interest in Margaret shortly. She would not sleep with him and that would end it for sure. Irmgard shrugged, Margaret would nurse a broken heart for a little while and then life would go on. She would get over it; all girls eventually did.

Margaret had indeed a great time at the fair. She was instantly in love for the first time in her life. She had always thought that particular phenomenon happened only to other girls, and now it had caught up with her at last. She could not believe what had happened. She had caught the eye of the most eligible bachelor in town. When Bernhard had pulled her to his table, she had felt the envy of every girl present. Margaret, the most modest of all females, felt a twinge of pride in herself for having Bernhard Dreier interested in her.

When Bernhard brought her home that night, he attempted to kiss her, but she gently pulled back. It was too quick she told him; they barely knew each other. So she took his hand, looked deeply into his eyes, and then raced up the steps to her parents' house. Bernhard was too stunned to even feel insulted.

The next day, her mother noticed that Margaret was dreamy and absent minded. This was not particular unusual for Margaret, but the low humming of a popular song was. For once, Ruth noted, it was not a church song. So, while they were in the kitchen snapping beans for supper, Ruth asked if Margaret if she had a good time at the fair the previous day.

Margaret's eyes looked so happy that Ruth was taken aback. Wow, she thought, Margaret is in love at last. Now I can only hope that he is a good man. Ruth looked at her daughter encouragingly.

"Tell me about him child," Ruth went on snapping beans while she waited for an answer. Conversations with Margaret were always testing her patience, but for once she was too curious to mind it.

"Mama," Margaret began, "his name is Bernhard Dreier. He works at a metal plant in the next village. He is twenty-five years old and he is such a good-looking man. He is funny and charming and all the girls are in love with him. He danced only with me last night. I will see him again on Saturday. Oh Mama, I am so excited."

Upon her daughter's description of the man, Ruth was not worried for she knew how this would end. Margaret would have her puppy love for a few weeks at the most and then this Casanova would get bored with her. Her daughter would suffer a major heart break and then would insist on entering a convent. Ruth was not worried about her daughter's virginity either. She knew Margaret well enough; no matter how this guy would try, Margaret was too much of a Catholic to give in to such sinful behavior. People did not know this about her, Ruth thought, but behind that accommodating exterior was a stubborn streak. Sometimes in her quiet moments Ruth was worried about Margaret. She was stubborn alright but also extremely fragile. She cried easily and mostly over matters that Ruth did not fully understand. There was a need in Margaret that was foreign to Ruth. This strange need for hugs and kisses, Ruth sensed it, but was unable to fulfill that need in her daughter. Ruth was just not familiar with that concept; in the aftermath of the war it was considered a weakness.

All week Margaret remained on cloud nine. She was in a trance and when Saturday finally came, she was exalted. After she had done her chores, she went upstairs to dress. This was her first date with a man. She chose a pretty print dress that hugged her curves without being too revealing. White low-heeled pumps completed the outfit. She even applied a little lip stick. As the last touch she grabbed her purse and was on her way.

It was a forty-five-minute walk to the old mill where they were supposed to meet. Margaret was full of anticipation. She could hardly breathe at the prospect of seeing Bernhard again. When she arrived at last at the location, she was ten minutes early. Good, she thought, then I have time to collect myself.

Three o'clock came and went. So he is a little late, no big deal, she said to herself. At fifteen minutes passed three, she figured her watch was fast. At half passed, she thought he may have missed his bus, and was waiting for the next one. At four o'clock she started to worry a little. What if he had forgotten her? Or maybe it was her fault; yes, that was likely it. She had gotten the date wrong. Of course, How could she blame him? Their date was next Saturday and she had gotten it mixed up. It was so typical of her. After she had waited for two hours, she went back home. She was so disappointed that she cried. Then she berated herself for her own foolishness. She could not blame this on him. If she was so stupid and gotten the dates wrong, she had no one to blame but herself. Ruth saw her coming and knew right away that she had cried. Poor thing, she thought. Either they had an argument or what was more likely he had not shown up. Whatever it was, it was better this way. Nothing good could come out of that relationship and it was best severed before it began. It would save Margaret pain later on.

Margaret remained gloomy all week and did her chores on auto pilot. She ate a lot of sugar; a habit she had developed as a young child. Whenever she felt overwhelmed or sad or depressed, she ate raw sugar by the spoon. It was the only drug available to her and would turn out to be a lifelong addiction.

A surprise was in store for Margaret when Saturday finally came. She was about to feed the chickens at eight o'clock in the morning when she bumped into Bernhard totally unexpected. She nearly dropped the bowl of chicken feed and her mouth fell open in shock.

"Good morning my beautiful child," he said gallantly.

"Good morning to you," stammered Margaret, trying to recover from the shock. Bernhard looked at her with his most impertinent grin.

"Let's have a cup of coffee at your house," he asserted proudly, "better yet, let's have breakfast." Bernhard had no problem inviting himself to Margaret's house. This was somewhat the custom in those days and not exactly unusual.

Ruth had seen her daughter and Bernhard through the window. Oh god, she thought upon seeing him. He is the wrong man for Margaret in every way. She had not yet spoken a word with him and yet she was sure. He was too good looking and too self-assured, Ruth thought. No this will never do. Hopefully this thing will die its natural death soon.

While they were having coffee, bread, and sausage for breakfast, Margaret asked timidly if she had gotten the date mixed up last Saturday. She said that she had waited for two hours and then walked home. Bernhard looked at her in amusement.

"No, my treasure, you have not gotten the date wrong. I had a soccer game. It was very important and I had forgotten all about our date. I hope you were not too sad about my not showing up."

"No," said Margaret quickly, "I just wanted to make sure."

There was no apology or regret in his voice. He was busy and had not shown up for their date. If she had waited two hours that was her problem. It was just that simple.

They had a wonderful time at breakfast and Margaret told herself that he had made up for the missed date. They went on a walk afterward and Bernhard kissed her when they entered the wooded area. Margaret had never been kissed like that before. Sure, this was not her first kiss. But this was a real kiss, not a peck on the cheek. It excited her as much as it scared her. When he forced his tongue into her mouth she was shocked for a moment.

An avalanche of feeling flooded through her body. Bernhard could sense her inexperience and it aroused him. He was delighted. This girl, this gorgeous young lady, was actually a virgin and she was his for the picking. It was incredible. Oh, he would have great fun with her. He would be her first. When Bernhard deposited Margaret back to her house that night, she was in seventh heaven. Her mother saw it with astonishment, but no alarm bells were ringing just yet. So that date had gone well. Why not a little fun for Margaret, she deserved it. When the end of this relationship came, and it would, that was for certain, she would have the heartaches, but that was better than a marriage with this man. But rest assured that would never happen.

Ruth would be wrong about this. The relationship did continue. Maybe due to Margaret's strong Catholic beliefs not to have sex before marriage she unwittingly forced Bernhard's hand. He could not have her any other way and so in the end he proposed to her. Margaret was elated and Ruth was horrified at the news. It was Ruth this time, who asked Margaret in desperation, about her plans on becoming a nun.

Margaret laughed, "Mama, I have totally changed my mind about that. I do not want to become a nun. That was just a mood of mine. It seems ridiculous now that I ever thought that was my calling."

Ruth's heart sank. She had a very bad feeling about this union. However, she was not a woman who told her children what to do. She had always believed in letting them live their own lives and she was not about to interfere now. She remembered the day Margaret had introduced Bernhard to her. Ruth had felt the condescending look from him and had not liked it. He thought of her and Margaret's family as inferior. She did not mind that because it was not important enough for her. Plus, she was not the one who had to deal with him; therefore, what he thought of her did not matter much. But now he was marrying Margaret and Ruth felt an oncoming doom.

She also remembered that Margaret had bruises on her face on several occasions during their courtship. She had pressed her for an explanation, but Margaret was vague and had tried to downplay the issue. Once they had had the following conversation. Ruth had asked Margaret point blank about her bruised face. Margaret was not happy about the direct question by her mother.

"I made a stupid mistake, Mama. It was really all my fault. I won't do it again."

Ruth looked at her inquiringly and asked, "And what mistake did you make, child?"

"Oh mom, I danced with another man, and I should not have done that. I know Bernhard cannot stand that, so I had it coming. I should have known that it made him jealous."

Ruth's face took on a serious expression. She asked Margaret to sit down and looked at her daughter sharply. She gathered her thoughts and then began to speak in measured tones.

"Margaret you are my daughter and I love you. I am going to do something I very seldom do. I will give you something that everybody needs from time to time, but no one likes to take."

"Oh mom," Margaret interrupted, "You are giving me a lecture. Please don't."

"No not a lecture, but a piece of advice," said Ruth desperately.

"Don't marry this man, my dear. If he hits you before you are even married, he will continue to do so. And don't think you can change a man. Women always think that, the foolish ones anyway. It never happens. If he is that possessive before you've even stepped in front of the altar, there is no telling what he is capable of after you say 'I do.' When you say yes, your fate is sealed. You know the Catholic laws as well as I do. Far be it from me to tell my children what to do, but in this case, I'll make an exception. Don't marry him Margaret, I am warning you; you will make the biggest mistake of your life."

"Oh Mama," Margaret laughed, "I have never heard you talking like this. You are definitely not a drama queen, but today you are coming close. He did not mean it. I made him angry is all. I should have known he is overly sensitive when it comes to me looking in another men's direction. It was no big deal and I provoked it."

"I see he has brainwashed you already and my words are not falling on fertile ground," Ruth said with resignation, "I still harbor the hope that you will change your mind eventually. Just give my words some consideration. That is all I ask of you."

Margaret laid her hand on Ruth's shoulder.

"Mama, there is nothing to consider. He loves me and I love him. We will get married and we will have a family and everything will be alright. I will be so happy; you will see Mama."

Ruth shrugged her shoulders. It was useless, she thought. She wanted to shake her daughter. She wanted to yell for once. She thought, child, does he love you? Really? What kind of love is that when he hits you before you haven even give your marriage vows? She said nothing more though; it was Margaret's life not hers.

They were getting married the first week in August. It was agreed that they would first live in a small house on Margaret's parents' estate. Meanwhile both the groom and the bride's parents had agreed to pay for a down payment on a house of their own. They would live in Bernhard's little town. Bernhard's parents would occupy the upper floor unit of the house so they could help with the mortgage by paying rent. That was an absolute necessity, since the mortgage was higher than what Bernhard earned. I wonder what it felt to him, being so deep in debt. He was not familiar with gratefulness, so he did not overly thank his or my mother's parents for the help with the down payment. He felt that he was entitled to it anyway. Being grateful was a concept Bernhard Dreier had never mastered, not even on his death bed.

Chapter 5

The Hurting of the Soul

"Emotional wounds change people, experiencing pain transforms us psychologically" (Psychofactz.tumblr.com)

I wonder when my mother's illness of schizophrenia actually began. I do agree with science that it has its origins in genetics and environment. The genetics may have come from my grandfather, who was not schizophrenic in my view, but anti-social. My mother's childhood may have had something to do with it as well. The isolation and the constant work. She really did not have a chance to develop her own personality. Plus, she was a girl and as such did not get the respect that her brothers had.

Her environment had not gotten better with her marriage. As a matter of fact, it got worse. If she thought she had successfully escaped the milieu of her childhood, she was quickly disillusioned. I wonder how long it took for her to deeply regret not becoming a nun. At first, she must have thought it would all work out. She would overcome her husband's anger with tenderness and giving him a child. Never in her wildest dreams did she think that she would now be placed completely in her husband's cage of fear, rage, control, and brutality for the next fifty years.

My mother got pregnant immediately after she got married. My father was ecstatic. I do know now that he was thrilled not so much that he had a healthy child, but as previously mentioned, when I listed the symptoms of narcissism, to integrate a baby into his court. His kingdom would be expanded.

In any case the pregnancy went off without a hitch. My father had refrained from beating her too badly during those nine months. He still hit her, but not as severely. Margaret excused his behavior. He was under a lot of stress, was her excuse for him. He switched to verbal abuse during the time of my mother's pregnancy. From what I experienced later, I thought the verbal abuse was worse than the hitting. But what did I know? My mother was the one who got the brunt of his fury and harm in that area. I wonder, and not for the first time, how much of a mother's anxiety affects the baby in her womb. If in fact the baby can sense the mother's distress, then my brother and me had to live with fears even before we were even born. Being born into such an unstable situation had repercussions for my brother and me.

Nine months after the doomed marriage had taken place had taken place, Margaret gave birth to a child. Her daughter was born in May of 1965. Margaret now mistakenly thought that this child would save her troubled marriage.

During her pregnancy she had prayed for a healthy child and her prayers were answered. She had given birth to a beautiful baby girl. While she recovered from the birth and stayed three days in a hospital, her husband was delighted. He was on his best behavior. He brought her flowers and candy. He reassured her that he was proud of her and that he loved her. She basked in the praise and hoped that his sweetness toward her would last. It is clear to me now that he actually was ecstatic at that moment to have a healthy child, a continuation of himself.

When she was released from the hospital, Margaret was overjoyed. She had given Bernhard a rosy cheeked baby girl and he adored her again, just like at their first meeting. Bernhard had taken a week off from work. Margaret soon found out that her husband's new found tenderness did not last. He criticized her every move after her hospital stay was completed. She held the baby wrong when she bathed her, she did not change the diapers correctly, and she fed the baby the bottle too fast. Margaret, still exhausted from the birth, was glad when he went back to work. Having him around the house all the time was pure torture. Constant fatigue was Margaret's companion.

In addition to that, there was the ever-present tension of pleasing her husband and never quite achieving that. She could not recognize that there was no way to satisfy a narcissist. And so, it was a never-ending dance for her. She tried tenderness and submission but of course it was never enough. She attempted to fulfill his every wish. She kept the house clean. She did not ask for household money even if it meant begging food from her parent's farm. She waited up for him when he came back late at night from his bar hopping, where he spent their nonexistent money. Of course, now that she had a child, it was her responsibility to keep the baby quiet when he was present.

Margaret was under constant pressure not to disturb her husband. Not so easy when you have an infant and a sick, perfectionist husband. No wonder she developed schizophrenia. She had fragile nerves to begin with, and with that husband anyone would have problems.

My mother had attempted to describe her feelings to me years later. She said she felt that Bernhard did not care if she had food on the table for the children as long as she had it ready for him when he was home. He did not care that she was alone with the children all day and many a night as long as he had his bar parties.

My father saw my mother as his personal slave. She had to cater to his needs of which there were many. He required her to be there for him day and night. If he came home late at night, he expected her to be up and put up with his ranting and raving. During the day, it was her duty to keep the house neat and clean, and he had rigorous standards in this matter. God forbid she fell below expectation on this matter. She had to cook his meals and heaven forbid she had put too little or too much salt on the potatoes. The laundry had to be done to his specifications. Heaven help her if there were still wrinkles on his shirts. On top of all that he expected loving tenderness from her. Alas, even a lady like my mother, who basically adored her husband, had to have cracks in her worship.

She also felt that he was angry with her for some reason. He had told her that she was too fat after the baby's birth. So, she tried to diet. It was a hopeless case. She was so depressed that her preferred drug was sugar. She ate it raw by the spoon when she had no money for flour and eggs to bake cookies. Of course, the enormous sugar consumption did not help her figure. She grew more and more out of proportion. This fact did not help her depression. She felt she had lost the one asset that had attracted her husband. It also diminished her sex drive. Of course, she was obliged to perform in her marriage bed, that was the Catholic law, but it was increasingly hard for her to do so. When a husband is physically, emotionally, and verbally abusive, a wife is not happy to have sex with him, even one who was as devoted as my mother.

I imagine my mother was very desperate at the time to keep her Catholic vows and not fall apart. She spent more and more time in prayer. She began to avoid social functions and did not go grocery shopping when she had telling bruises on her face. As is the case with most victims of domestic violence, she became very isolated.

When I was only seven-month-old, Margaret discovered that she was pregnant again. She was horrified about this second pregnancy and the shock was great. She had refused to take birth control but Bernhard had promised to be careful. And now she was going to have a second baby. The first one would not even be eighteen months old by the time she had baby number two. How would she be able to handle that work load? It was absolutely terrifying to her. Now she had to bathe two babies, feed two babies, and diaper two babies. Plus, keep the house clean, cook, do the grocery shopping, stay up for nightly abuses, and diet to get her figure back after birth.

If all of that was not enough, Margaret's mother-in-law, Gerda, put her two cents in. Her husband's mother told my mother bluntly that she could not afford a second child. She made it sound like her precious son had nothing to do with Margaret's new pregnancy. It was all Margaret's fault of course.

My poor mother, at the age of twenty-three, she now had two children, her mother-in-law's scorn, and her body would go through the enormous changes of pregnancy again. Her husband was actually not thrilled about this new pregnancy either. He called her a breeding cow and feared that the neighbors would agree with his mother's view and he would be the laughing stock in town. Of course, he had no sympathy for her condition and did not appreciate how draining a pregnancy actually is. All he cared about was his reputation, his inconvenience, and the additional cost another baby would bring. There would be even less money for partying now. It frustrated him immensely that he did not have enough money to party as it was, but with a second baby that would be even more restricted. Margaret had displeased him tremendously with this second pregnancy. She would pay for that, that much was certain.

Margaret herself was terrified at the prospect of a second child. She had no support system in place. In fact, she was the scapegoat. Everyone was mad at her and she had the burden and the responsibility. Not to mention, the exhaustion. She felt trapped. So, she prayed. She heard voices for the first time. Not very often, only in times of extreme stress.

By September, her second child was delivered. It was a boy and she named him Mark. He was a big baby, exactly nine pounds. Margaret was exhausted from the delivery. Labor had been induced, and she felt terribly tired. This time Bernhard was less attentive to her. He had wanted a son to be sure, but not quite so soon. She had gotten the timing wrong and of course it was all her fault.

Margaret was chronically exhausted, both hysically and emotionally. She had to deal with two babies, both of them under two years old. She was constantly feeding, bathing, changing diapers, trying to keep the house clean, go grocery shopping when she had the money, do laundry, and pray.

While Margaret was exhausted, her husband was cranky, hostile, and incredibly selfish. He expected her to attend to him, cook his meals on time, serve him coffee, and iron his shirts. And god forbid she did not do a good job ironing, then all hell would break lose. He never had a kind word for her. He called her a fat pig and accused her of spending too much money on the household. But, the lord help her, there was never any money to spend. He did not care that he did not provide any money, he only cared that they lacked it. There was no money to clothe her babies. She was glad that her cousin provided hand me downs from her children and toys as well.

The nights when he came home drunk were the worst. He was hostile and so brutal to her on those nights. She lived in deep fear of them. He would come home and she would be terrified when she heard the doorbell around one or two o'clock. She had been sleeping on and off by then, comforting her son Mark and soothing Susan from her nightmares. The minute she opened the door for Bernhard she fought with an anxiety attack.

She hastily tried to cover her panic by saying, "Bernhard, it is good to see you! Come in."

He looked at her with bloodshot eyes and said drunkenly, "Shut up you fat, useless cow. You have ruined my life. Two screaming brats, a fat ugly wife, that's what I have to deal with every day."

He hit her then hard and heavy. When she fell to the ground he kicked her in the ribs. The pain took her breath away.

All the while Bernhard was yelling from the top of his lungs, "You stupid, hideous bitch who is good for nothing. You cannot even please your man." And then more blows came.

And my mother brokenly pleaded, "Please, please don't hit me Bernhard," she cried. "I will be better, I promise." And then she wept with broken sobs.

When my father's attacks on her stopped, he fell exhausted into bed. My mother slept on the couch, crying herself to sleep. Her face was puffy from the blows and her eyes would be black by morning. But nightly horror or not, she had to feed her babies in the morning, serve her husband his meals, clean the house, and listen to her mother-in-law's insults. Not to mention laundry and ironing. Margaret felt like she was in a trance. She would avoid going outside the house; with those bruises on her face that was quite out of the question. She was lonely and sad, hopeless, and completely overworked. A deep depression settled inside of her. Praying as often as possible seemed to ease the pain a little. Prayer seemed all that she had left and even that was resented by her husband. It took time away from her chores, and she never seemed to get them all done these days. It must have been that Bernhard felt the prayers took time away from her attention to him, which he craved, even if he did mistreat her. She was his property and had to please him at all times. She was doing less of it these days and that made him even more angry towards her. It is amazing how the narcissist mind works. They keep their wives as prisoners and expect them to be grateful for the privilege.

My grandmother has told me that my mother confided in her about her marriage. She in turn related the accounts to me. I asked her how she had felt when my mother told her what was going on.

She said the following: "Child, in those days things were different. When a marriage was as bad as your parents', it would still most likely not end in divorce. First of all, there is the church. The Catholic church does not permit divorce. In this family everybody is Catholic. Your mothers-in-laws would be scandalized by a divorce. They would blame your mother for the shame she brought to the family. Your father might kill her if she even suggested such a thing."

"Oh grandma, that is such an old-fashioned drama. Mama is unhappy. I am quite sure God would forgive her if she chose to divorce. And you have yet to answer where you stand on the issue."

She looked at me thoughtfully for a long time, "Child, I was born in 1918. I was told marriage is forever. This was my family's motto. But being a somewhat modern woman, I agree with you. God would have likely forgiven your mother if she had gotten divorced in her case. But the divorce itself would not solve the problem. How would your mother live? She has never worked and I am not sure she could survive in any job. Her nerves are not very strong as it is and I think your father has weakened them further. In addition to that, I do not think your mother could parent you properly. Now child hold on, I know what you are going to say. You think the two of them together have done an extremely poor job of it. I cannot disagree with that. Neither one of your parents were cut out for parenting and together they were even worse. I am just saying, your mother was incapable of taking care of her children, even I was going to help her. I hate to say it child, but your mother needed more care than I could ever give her. Me taking her and her two little children in was a task I did not want to try. And yes, I would not like to be the subject of society's judgement. I did care about what people would say about my family and me. There is an element of shame to it and I admit I did not want to face it. That said, I would have offered her shelter had she asked for it."

An element of shame, I thought. I honestly did not understand how they could be shamed by other people. I thought, even as a very young child, that shame belonged in my family first and foremost. There was all this brutality going on behind closed doors, all the insults, all the various abuses. God in his heaven, I thought, must be ashamed to the core by this so called family. They judged every family in town, but my god take a good look at their own? Never. In my mind, my family was the worst. How dare they criticize anyone? It seemed inconceivable to me. It stunned me and angered me.

Because I felt that way, I was very conflicted as a child. I developed a haze that I later identified as hate. And the person I hated the most was myself.

Chapter 6

Susan ages 4-6

Helpless

"What a terrible feeling to love someone and not be able to help them" (Jennifer Niven)

I am now writing on the account of my own memories. At four years old, I was so grateful and happy that I had a little brother. We were only sixteen months apart, almost like twins.

In many ways we were inseparable. We can only thank the universe that we had each other in this crazy upbringing we experienced.

My brother and I talked recently, and he told me that he felt the same way. We at least had each other in this horrendous childhood. We helped each other out when we were able. We played for hours in harmony and peace while our father was at work. As long as he was not in the house we could forget the tension and even our mother relaxed for a while. She was relieved from entertaining us because we did that ourselves and that gave her a much needed break. Whenever she had a minute, she would spend her time in prayer. We were too young to recognize the desperation of our mother. But we found resilience by forgetting the world for a while through play.

Looking back now, I do understand how difficult my mother's situation was. Her husband was spending the little money he earned in bars. He partied, flirted with other women at the very least, and got very aggressive when he got home. He brutally assaulted my mother in his drunken, piss poor mood. He blamed her for his lack of money even though she never spent a dime on herself. He blamed her for the second pregnancy which came too quickly after the first. He blamed her when she was happy. He blamed her for everything. He isolated her and got extremely jealous when anyone paid her any attention.

He was further fueled by the hatred his mother had for my mom. Her living in the unit above us was pure poison for my mother. She was consumed with jealousy and envy of my mom. She resented her beauty, her sweetness, and her popularity. Plus, she encouraged her son's beatings on his wife. This stoking of my father's fire proved to be so brutal for my mother.

The tension was terrible not only for my mother, but also for my brother and me. We learned early on that when our father was around we were harshly penalized for every mistake. We learned to fear to answer wrong, even to think wrong. This would impact us for the rest of our lives.

My brother and I were not aware of my parents' mental conditions, but we did sense that something was not right. I learned that in my father's presence it was very costly if I made any misstep. The punishment was so harsh. I feared the belittlement and humiliating remarks that came from the slightest mistakes. A glass of spilled milk could turn instantly into a disaster.

My mother gave us plenty of hugs, but there was no substance in them. No protection or confidence. She could not guide us because she had no power. We saw her as just another member of the household who was afraid of our father. I do feel, however, that even those substance-lacking hugs gave us some feeling of being loved. In the end I am very grateful to her for giving us some tenderness and recognition. I feel now that those hugs saved my brother and me from total bitterness.

In time my mother withdrew more and more into herself. Hopelessness, desolation, and exhaustion dominated her very existence. As her schizophrenia developed, she shut down emotionally and became more fanatic about prayers.

Growing up, fear was the dominant emotion my brother and I felt. Fear and a hate toward my father. I hated the fear he created, and I hated him for the brutal treatment of my mother. At a very early age, I had learned to hate and that hate inside of me hurt. It conflicted me terribly. I was too young to recognize the hate, and therefore it created emotional pain.

Seeing my mother in pain fueled my agony. In some ways it paralyzed me emotionally. My helplessness to relieve her stress wounded me deeply. I may have been barely five years old, but I already knew what it meant to be injured. I knew words hurt, and I had seen my mother's body covered in bruises and the black eyes on her face.

I heard her begging my father for mercy when he came home drunk and brutal. I stood by my door and cried until there were no tears left. I was disgusted at myself for not opening that door. I tore my hair out for being too cowardly to step in. I heard her begging him not to hurt her and my heart was torn to pieces.

The revulsion I felt for myself was so deep it broke me. I slapped myself for not having the guts to help. Those nights of brutality were not few and far between. They came with regularity.

I developed a deep hate for my father, my mother, and most of all for myself. I hated my father for hurting my mother and the horrible screaming that was associated with the beating. I hated my mother for allowing it and myself for not interfering. It was a vicious cycle.

Witnessing your mother's degradation and humiliation at such an early age is a bad thing for a child. Of course, I was told that all that is going on in this house must be kept secret. Even a child knows that when something must be kept secret that it is shameful. Shame is one of the lowest emotion anyone can have. I had so much to be ashamed of as a child that it became a way of life for me.

If it had to be secret, that meant that other people did not approve of it. That made perfect sense to me. How could they possibly approve of that horror? It also made me feel the shame was on myself. They would judge my father, and me too, for not having the guts to put a stop to it.

Of course, I now know that I was not to blame, but I could not see that at the time. I felt I should be ashamed of myself as well. I let my father beat up my mother and did not do anything to help her. Yes, the shame was mine too, to be sure. Thinking back, I'm not sure if the beating or the yelling was worse. The horrendous things he screamed at her. The tone of his voice was so very ugly. He called her a whore, stupid, dumb, a fat cow, and many other words that robbed her of her dignity. To block out the screaming, I stuck my fingers so deep in my ears that it hurt.

All the while, I stood at my door, sobbed silently, nearly choked on my tears, shook wildly, and imagined the worst images possible. Since religion was very present in my life, and I marched to church every Sunday, I knew the Bible stories well. My visions took me to Mount Sinai. I imagined my father tied up at the cross. I stood in front of him slapping him until my arm got tired. When I finally cried myself to sleep, I slept the sleep of exhaustion. The following mornings were not better. I saw my mother's swollen face and her puffy black eyes. The pain in them took my breath away.

While my father was sleeping off his previous intoxication, my brother and I were depressed. I often wondered if my father's violence was due to my misbehaving. I made a real effort to do better in order to spare my mother.

My mother did not make things easier by advising my brother and me to stay outside of our bedroom door. One time I had opened the door with a loud noise in order to distract my father. My mother had a serious talk with me the next day.

"Susan," she said sternly, "no matter what you hear at night, you must never ever open that door. That would make things even worse."

She looked at me with her puffy painful face and said, "You cannot help me."

Her words made me feel powerless and so very sad. It is hard to put into words what those events do to a child. When fear and shame rule in your formative years it creates a block. You get secrecy hammered into your brain from your father and your mother. My mother was terrified that I would tell anyone what was going on. She did not need to worry. Shame sat so deep in my soul already; I would not tell anyone. I also feared my father's wrath. I was too much of a coward to tell a soul. No need to even swear me to secrecy.

This is why most children will not report sexual abuse or physical abuse either. Their parents do not need to tell them to keep silent. They get brainwashed into thinking it is their shame to bear, and so often as a result they stay mute.

Chapter 7

Susan ages 6-8

Security Breach

"There is no greater blessing than a family hand that lifts you from a fall; but there is no greater curse than a family hand that strikes you when you're down" (Wess Fessler).

When I was six years old, it occurred to me for the first time that all people in my family have gone crazy. Starting with my father. I did not know exactly what was wrong with him, but something had to be. One could not be that mean by nature. Perhaps that was insanity. My mother meanwhile had begun to hear noises that no one else heard. She began to see ghosts everywhere, and while that did not frighten me, it was weird nonetheless. My grandmother on my father's side was also insane in my mind. Gerda had an obsession with rosaries. Her giant rosary hung over the television in her living room. She had us praying for my father's immortal soul and I found that quite unbalanced. I thought, God would forgive anyone, but only if they repent. And I had yet to see that from my father or my grandmother.

This realization at six years old drew some giggles from me. I lived in a house filled with maniacs and if it wasn't so brutal it would be downright funny. Amidst the terror, it was possible to have some comic relief in this house. The drama in our house was as cruel as it was hilarious. The domestic violence was heartbreaking and shook me to the core, nothing funny about that. It made me cry and hurt so deeply. My mother's ghosts were kind of funny though. In her mind they popped up everywhere, sat down on her chairs, occupied the telephone, hid in her closet, and were present in faucets and water heaters. My grandmother's nonsense was neither scary nor funny to me, it was annoying. Forced prayers for my father inspired me to reword my conversations with God. I asked him for forgiveness that he had to witness such phony requests.

Religion was, as I stated before, a major component in my house. My relationship with it became distorted from an early age. Everybody used it to rectify their position. For my mother, it was comfort and mercy. For my father, it was a guarantee that he would not be punished too hard. No matter what he did, if he sat in church every Sunday, he could receive eternal life. My grandmother used it for deals with God so she could have her wishes fulfilled. In my mind, God was in his heaven, listened to all this rubbish, and smiled at the sheer foolishness. That does not mean I felt superior to everyone in the house. I had my doubts about my own sanity as well at times, especially when I dissolved into giggles unexpectedly when I contemplated all the nonsense that was going on in my life.

At seven years old I had an incident that was connected to the church that confused the hell out of me. It was not a painful experience, but in many ways, I found it extremely puzzling and bewildering. Ever since I had learned to read, I had a passion for books. They were so much part of my life. Books could transport me away from the world I was in. I could pretend I was a heroine, cry over the misfortune of some person, or laugh at a funny anecdote. There was only one library in our little town, and that was the Catholic library located right next to the church.

Here I sat and read many days on the bench under the big chestnut tree. I often brought a bag of cookies and a jug of juice with me and forgot time, engrossed in books. On those occasions I was truly happy, exchanging reality for a fantasy world.

One raining autumn day, I decided to take the fifteen-minute walk from my house to the library to borrow a book. In those days it was perfectly okay for a seven-year-old to roam the streets alone. When I reached the library, I selected a few children books, checked them out, and was about to head home. The altar boy, Hubert Klaussen, stopped me. He was sixteen years old and had an impeccable reputation. He looked at me kindly and had a friendly smile on his face.

Hubert said, "Susan come into the church with me for a moment."

"No time Hubert, I have to go home and anyway today is not Sunday," I replied.

Hubert gently grabbed my arm, "All your friends are in there, Annegret, Dora, and others."

This made me curious. Why were they in church on a weekday? My curiosity got the better of me and I followed him into the cathedral. Inside the church it was cool and I saw my friends huddling by the confessional. I was surprised and perplexed. What was going on, I wondered.

Then Hubert made a very strange request. He asked us to line up in front of the confessional and pull our panties down. This completely puzzled me. I was stunned and bewildered but not really frightened. All the girls did as they were told, me included. It seemed as if we were all in a trance. At the age of seven, I am sure none of us comprehended this ritual, especially since a very respected altar boy was giving us the instructions. After all, we were programmed to think that the Catholic church could do no wrong. Therefore, we never objected to anything that was done in this holy place. We paraded one by one in front of Hubert and he touched us lightly on our privates. Then we pulled up our panties and left the church. We went on our separate ways and did not talk about the strangeness of the situation.

When I reached the hill top that was not far from my house, I stopped. I looked down at the wildflowers and the rough terrain of the hill and felt the whole incident had a surreal quality. I was never going to talk about it, that was for sure. The very idea was out of the question. With whom anyway? My friends had been all present at the strange occasion. My mother? That was a laugh. She would punish me and threaten me with eternal hellfire because her sacred church was not capable of any wrongdoing. My father? He would be the last person on earth I would confide in. Even if I had people I could talk to it would have been unlikely for me to actually unburden myself to anyone. The subject matter was just too weird.

I had already learned about shame in my family. Domestic violence, secrets, and my mother telling me not to question or interfere with my father. No, Hubert did not have to swear us to secrecy. In this town that hid shameful events, no one was going to talk. The incident left me strangely shaken. Even now as a mature adult I can recall it clear as a bell.

Meanwhile, my mother's schizophrenia became more profound. She had strange periods that the doctor called episodes. I came home from school one day and all the closets were open, sheets, clothes, towels, everything was piled in heaps all over the house. In the bath tub swam my mother's winter coat, the washing machine was working nonstop, and the clothesline outside was tightly occupied with a variety of garments soaking in the pouring rain.

My father's ugly voice was roaring and I could hear him well before I reached the house. He was shouting on the top of his lungs.

"Margaret, you stupid cunt, all the neighbors are talking and laughing about us. You are shaming me in front of everyone with your dumb behavior. Don't you know it is raining and that the wash is getting soaked?"

My mother ignored him and went on with her task and hung more of the wash outside. She was completely oblivious to the rain.

One must picture this. My father yelling on top of his lungs at my mother, who, ignoring him completely, went on with her chore. She was wet to the bone, but continued to hang more and more stuff outside into the driving rain.

Oh Jesus, I could not take this any longer. I went into my room, sat on my bed, and laughed. I laughed until I was breathless and tears were streaming down my face. My belly hurt from all the laughter. Every time I thought I was back in control, I looked out of the window and saw my mother hanging more items outside into the driving rain. Then my father's voice screaming at the top of his lungs. I could not decide if this was a comedy or a drama.

The irony of the whole situation occurred to me. Here was my father, who beat up and entrapped his wife, talking about shame. He should be ashamed, I thought furiously. After all, there was no harm in hanging the wash outside in a rain storm. She did not hurt anyone. And so what if people laughed? I laughed, too. Laughing was a good thing after all. Why should one be ashamed about that?

That was my perception on the matter when I was seven years old. I do think that perception was quite sensible. I think that even now as I am a grown and mature adult.

Up until this point, my mother had still harbored a worship for my father. He may hurt her, insult her, and enslave her, but none of these reasons were strong enough to stop my mother from still adoring him.

In the end, however, he did something that finally tipped the scale. He did the one thing that my mother would not forgive. He cheated on her. I am trying to understand what went on in my mother's head when she found out. I have interviewed and asked her as an adult about her feelings on that matter. It was a very interesting conversation.

Me: "Mom, how did you found out that he was cheating on you?"

Mom: "Everyone in town knew, the neighbors told me, and my friends."

Me: "And how did you feel?"

Mom: "Insulted and hurt. The woman was more than ten years older than me. That made it worse."

At this point I was surprised. No word about love; just injured vanity and hurt pride as far as I could tell.

Then my mother said, "I sent my father, your grandfather, to talk with Bernhard."

This again drew laughter from me. Oh god, my taciturn grandfather. I pictured him in his Sunday's finest, climbing on the tractor on his way to visit my father to talk to him about holy matrimony and fidelity. I would have paid good money to be present during that conversation.

I do believe after my mother recovered from the first insult and hurt, she turned the matter around in her mind. She came to the conclusion that she had actually a weapon now. Adultery was strictly forbidden by Catholic law. She could not divorce her husband as that was still against the commandments. But now she could legally refuse him in bed.

Since she had very little desire for sex lately, she was now able to skip this pesky little chore completely.

Imagine a narcissist receiving the message from his wife that she no longer desires his presence in bed. Whether he still desires her or not does not matter. The fact of the matter is that this is an insult to him and a severe one. One must understand that deep down, it nags the narcissist to be refused by anyone, especially his own wife. He loses part of his control. He gets more aggressive than he already is. This little stunt of my mother would have grave consequences for me.

Shortly after my father's cheating scandal rocked our little community he was arrested for a DUI. He did some time in prison again, which was covered up as much as possible by my family. My brother and I were not troubled by the fact and we were secretly happy to be out of his reach for a while. In those days, I did not even know he was in prison. There was no social media, and children were not very interested in adult affairs. We were just glad not to see him for a while.

This put a financial strain on my mother, but I hardly felt it. We had always been poor whether he was in jail or at home. The advantage of him being in jail was that it created peace. Unfortunately, when his prison time was up, he was around again. It is important to note that my mother stood by him against the onslaught of gossip that his arrest had created. Not that he ever thanked her for that, of course.

After his "vacation", as always, he was not in a good mood. He tried to find people's weaknesses; it made him feel better. He had certainly found a way to put me down, and a very effective way, I might add.

In school I was a fairly good student, except for one subject. That subject was mathematics. I had difficulties with it even in elementary school. I felt really stupid, dumb, and ashamed that I was below average with numbers. My father had seen the D in mathematics on my report card. He immediately began to put me down and criticized my failings gleefully. On the days when he had graveyard shift he made it a point to restrict my playing time. He assigned me math problems and when I got them wrong he enjoyed my tears. It wasn't so much that I hated the practice, but the tension of being in my father's presence was so unbearable. He had found a flaw in me and was going to punish me for it so he could feel powerful and in charge. He would add a new terror for me at the age of eight.

Chapter 8

Susan age 8-10

Games and Power Play

"Around the world, we see the results of exploitation which destroys much…" (Pope John Paul II)

At the age of eight, I had developed a nervous stomach and sleepless nights. The ever present pressure had taken a toll on me. I was grateful when I did not hear the nightly doorbell bringing doom. I was grateful for uninterrupted sleep. I had developed nightmares, but talking to someone about them was out of the question. My mother would dramatize the matter with ghost stories and demons. My father was the very cause of those dreams. I had no person I could trust with those nightmares, so I tried to deal with them as best as I could by myself.

One night I woke up. I had a nightmare and was thirsty. I went in the kitchen to fetch a glass of water. I opened the kitchen door and froze. My father sat on a chair, his pants pulled down, and he was masturbating. I had never seen anyone do this before, and as soon as my paralyzed state allowed it, I ran out of the room. My heart was beating painfully in my chest and all I cared about was reaching the sanctuary of my room. Much to my horror my father had followed me.

His pants were still down and he had not bothered covering up. I remember wishing the floor would open up and swallow me. No such luck however.

My father looked at me strangely and said, "Susan, there is really no need to behave that way. Come over here and touch me."

No, no, no my mind screamed. Please oh please let me go! I was thinking these thoughts but no sound escaped my lips. I was shaking with terror. I think he knew it.

His next words were, "Come over here touch me and then I will leave."

I thought, he will leave. I will just touch him and he will leave. I wanted him to leave so badly. So, I went and touched him for one second, and mercifully, oh so mercifully he left. He left that night, but he came back. He requested more of my touch. I was completely horrified.

I did not understand it. I only knew I felt a terrible panic inside of me. I really did not want to do that. It took shame to new heights for me. Maya Angelou got it right when she said that sexual abuse is not only about power. Power is part of it, but what is so horrible is the sexual pleasure of the perpetrator. The grunting and the groaning. This is so shameful for the victim. The hideous excitement that no child should ever feel. That slippery undercoating of the oppressor. If your bully is your father, it is just too much to bear. When he is in a good mood, he buys you toys, kisses your cheeks, and hugs you. When he chooses to be a monster, he makes you touch his privates, beats your mother, yells at you, and puts you down.

I had to find a way to keep my sanity. I felt I was on the brink of losing my mind. And most of all I felt my depression. My recipe was nature. I found out that feeding horses was a way to calm me. I would gather some carrots and sugar cubes and took the thirty minutes' walk to the meadow where the horses were. Seeing them grazing peacefully brought a piece of heaven to my heart. The horses had the ability to lift my depression somehow. They would come to me and grab the carrots and sugar cubes from my hands with their smooth mouths and look at me with gentle eyes. Animals do not judge; maybe that is why I love them so much. It is believed that petting a furry friend brings medical benefits and I believe it.

As I got older, my family's situation had become more real to me. The sadness and anxiety were like a steady stream in my life. It seemed whenever saw a little light, darkness was sure to follow. Nature became my consolation and my resilience.

Nature gave me my strength back so that I could endure this life of tension and horror. In between my nature therapy, I began to contemplate if there was a way to get out of this situation. My age was the factor that I could not really escape. If only I could have a job. Could I get adopted? Not without my parent's permission, and rest assured I would never get that. I figured finally that I was halfway through this mess. In nine years, I would be eighteen and then come hell or high water, I would get out.

In the meantime, I would just have to find a way to survive it. Endure the domestic violence, endure the horrible confusion of the touching, and endure the constant tension in the house. I was also worried about my health lately. I was always vomiting, my stomach hurt, and I had terrible heartburn. Even at the age of nine I knew that the constant pressure was affecting me negatively.

I hated when I came back from my nature walk and faced the reality in my house. My mind went immediately under emotional strain. The sad thing is that, as a child, the situation was so confusing. Fathers are supposed to support and guide you, and in my case, he provided fear and oppression. Mothers are supposed to nurture you, and in my case, my mother provided distance and a world that no child can understand.

And you cannot run. To me, that was the worst. They will catch you and take you back home and then you as a child get punished. You really have no rights as a child. The parent has all the power. If you have a good person as a parent, you can come out fine. But if you have a narcissist, chances are, you will end up troubled. Especially in Germany, where the system is so slow and domestic issues are not really addressed.

I remember feeling so hopeless and helpless. I hated going home. There was always tension. It is hard to describe what constant stress feels like. You are never able to completely relax. There is always the notion: one wrong move and you are doomed. One wrong move can bring an avalanche of aggression and violence. Nelson Mandela got it right when he said, "It is the oppressor that defines the nature of the struggle."

It was hard for me to decide which abuse was the worst. The domestic violence that I witnessed made me feel guilty, uneasy, ashamed and deeply troubled. It fostered hate in me, even if I was only nine years old. The sexual abuse weighed heavily on me. It made me feel even more ashamed and burdened somehow. I think the desolation I felt was the worst. I didn't have anyone I could trust. I felt isolated and so alone in this.

I know now that all members of my family were victims. My mother was a victim of domestic violence and child labor, my father was a victim of a troubled upbringing and the condition of narcissism, and I was a victim of domestic violence, sexual abuse, verbal abuse, emotional abuse, and physical violence to some degree. No one in my family could come out of this mess whole.

I felt that I was nine years old and had already cried a lifetime of tears.

Chapter 9

Susan age 10-12

The Dark Hole

"We can easily forgive a child who is afraid of the dark; The real tragedy of life is when men are afraid of the light" (Plato)

Children have amazing resilience. When things are good for a moment, they take that moment and live happily in that short period of time. There were times when my family was almost normal. I cherished these moments. They were always short lived, but children are able to fill the tank of their soul on these brief moments. It helps them survive. When my brother and I played outside, we were able to forget our reality for a moment. We played ball, rode our bikes, and played in the nearby woods for hours. We were actually happy on those occasions of children entertainment.

It hurt me that I did not have a strong relationship with either of my parents. I had seen how my friends interacted with their parents and it pained me that I've never been able to obtain such a relationship with my father or my mother.

I was aware that my family was not the only one who had their troubles. A girl in my class, Angela, had a father who had committed suicide. He had hanged himself in a barn not far from my house. I had deep empathy for that girl. I saw her swollen eyes and I saw her hiding from the curious glances of teachers and children. I remember squeezing her hand one day and saying nothing. She looked at me sadly in her heartbreak and pain.

I remember hating the gossip that surrounded her. I always left the group when the subject of her father's suicide came up in school. In my own house the gossip about the suicide was alive and well. My grandmother on my father's side was in her element. She told everyone who would listen that the wife had cheated and that was the reason why the poor man had taken his life. I did not really listen to her glee because I had other worries. I had enough troubles as it was. I felt very sorry for Angela, but I had enough on my plate. I had cried for Angela and I was crying for myself. I thought, even if I cried for the whole world, it would not solve anything.

Then about two weeks after the incident with Angela's father, I came home from school and my mother was not present. This was not that unusual because she had a habit of leaving the house without notice. I remember I heard the doorbell ringing and I answered the door. My neighbor stood outside. I could tell she was very excited.

She told me, "Susan, your mother is in the barn."

I was flabbergasted. I asked confusedly, "What barn?"

"Why, the barn where that Marker girl's father hanged himself," she replied with ill-conceived excitement.

I did not know whether to laugh or to cry. Oh god, that is just great, I thought. Now I have to go into the damn barn and get her out. I tried to hide my fear of going into that building. Oh sweet Jesus, what next, I asked myself with apprehension. And so, we walked the short distance until we reached the barn. A group of people had formed outside the barn already, waiting with baited breath for the next developments.

I entered the haunted house and was actually terrified. The question in my head was making me so scared. What if my mother was hanging from the ceiling? It was not out of the question with my mother's erratic behavior. After all, one never knew how my schizophrenic mother would react. It was dark in the barn and at first, I could not see well. As I went further in, I suddenly saw a shape kneeling down at the end of the barn. It was my mother. She was praying. I approached her and asked her gently to come back out with me.

She looked at me like she was in a trance. In that moment I was intensely grateful that she had not hung herself. An understanding came into my mind. She was praying for the poor soul who had hung himself here. I better thank the Almighty that my mother was alive and well I thought. Angela, oh Angela, you poor girl. You have not found your father alive and well. I will be extra friendly to you from now on without being inquisitive and without ill-concealed curiosity.

My mother was docile as I led her out of the barn. She followed me without comment.

I tried to lighten the mood and said, "Mama, the next time you go into barns and pray for people's souls, could you try to avoid spooky ones? I am not particularly superstitious but this barn scared me."

She looked at me strangely and said, "You are cynical and you are way too young for it."

I thought, oh mama, if only you knew or could understand what is happening to me. Your illness, your husband molesting me, the domestic violence. I am so troubled, Mama. When we got back home, I was exhausted. I felt so tired. I should have done my homework but I seemed to have no energy. All I wanted was a good night sleep. That was not going to happen.

During that night my mother had an episode. She had taken a belt and was beating the stairs with it. She was chanting to drive the ghosts from the stairs. When I heard her, I closed my eyes and told myself it was better than a beating from my father.

My mother's schizophrenia had worsened over the years. My father called the doctor often and I could never make up my mind whether to laugh or to cry on such occasions. If my mother was aware that the doctor was on his way she would engage the whole household, including the doctor, in a delightful game of hide and go seek. She would hide in closets and under the bed. One time she even jumped out of a window. This window was, thank the lord, not too high from the ground. My amusement always faded when they caught her. Then they would tie her to the bed and inject her. Then my amusement turned to compassion.

I remember shortly after that event my mother had her first six-month hospital stay. I was horrified. Now my father would have full access to me. She had not been a great shield for my father's visits in my room, but now I had no shield at all.

I also thought that he might do worse to me than he already did. He had gradually increased his sexual demands since I was eight years old. First, he was satisfied with just touching. Then, I had to undress so he could touch me. I so wished I could vanish. When I was nine years old, he had left pornographic magazines in my room. I was disgusted by them as well as curious. At ten, he wanted me to take him in my mouth. I've never forgotten the time I performed that task. I choked and vomited. I cried. I rinsed my mouth with bleach afterward.

At ten years old, I saw the full force of controlling behavior that makes narcissists so malignant. It was my grandfather's birthday. He was turning seventy years old and was preparing for a big party. He would rent a venue and a band. There would be a big buffet and one hundred guests were invited. This was my grandfather on my father's side. He had always been a bright light in my life. His wife may have treated my mother horribly, but he didn't. And he was good to me as well. He regularly took me to church on Saturday nights and afterwards to his favorite pub. Once there, I was provided with a soda pop and peanuts. Plus, I would stand on a chair and played the slot machine. This was legal in Germany back then even for children. I was fascinated by pushing the bright red button whenever it lit up. Those evenings were my slice of heaven. They were my way of escaping my reality for a little while.

And now my beloved grandfather turned seventy years old. I was actually looking forward to this party. I still had some money from my latest babysitting job and had bought him a box of his favorite cigars. Such purchases presented no problems for children, because German laws did not prohibit minors from purchasing tobacco products.

The venue was wonderfully decorated with balloons and the band was playing. The buffet was set up and it looked wonderful. When I entered, the band was playing a popular hit and everyone was in a great mood. I got some food and a soda pop and began to relax. I chatted with people and I let my guard down. My mood dropped when I saw my father was approaching me. I went into defense mode. Please oh please do not let him spoil my day, I thought frantically.

He looked me up and down and I had come to hate that look. I did not want to deal with any kind of discomfort today. My mind was yelling from the inside, just go away, I am not in the mood for your stuff today. No such luck.

"Susan, come dance with me," he said smiling.

I do not know what on earth I was thinking, but I said no. How could I have been so stupid? I had no business saying no to my father if I wanted peace in my life. The minute I had said it I knew I was in trouble. I seemed to have forgotten rule number one in my life. You could never say no to my father. To him that was an insult and a rejection. I would have to pay for that no and I knew it. For some reason though, I was defiant. I just wanted to have a great day for once. I felt an unease come over me and it threatened to spoil my wonderful day. I tried to force that unpleasant thought from my mind but was only half successful.

Shortly after saying no to my father, I made another mistake that sealed my fate. This time it was my grandfather who asked me for a dance. I said yes. As I walked to the dancefloor with him, I literally felt my father's eyes stabbing into my back. After the dance I felt panic settled deep inside of me. I had made him mad. I would have to pay.

When I got home from the party he was waiting for me. He ordered me to come into the living room, where he sat on the couch. It felt like being in court. The verdict was already in as well. I was convicted. My father looked at me with those piercing eyes and got up from the couch. He did not say a word, but slapped me hard on the face. The blow was hard enough to make my nose and lips bleed. I tried to catch the blood with my hands forming a cup, but it fell to the floor anyway. I stood there shaking with fear and hated myself once more.

My father finally spoke to me, "Well, so you think you can reject me? Do you?"

I said nothing but tears were stinging in my eyes.

"Do you?" He repeated in that ugly cutting voice. "Answer me when I talk to you."

I found my voice finally and because I was afraid, I said, "I am sorry."

"Well," my father said finally, "let's see how sorry you are. Get a towel and clean the floor. You are making a mess with all your blood."

I mopped up the blood and hoped against hope that I would be dismissed. Of course, I had no such luck. My mother was in the kitchen and my father called her.

"Margaret," he said, "go to bed. I will be there later. First I need to discipline our daughter."

My mother gave me a look that was so sad that I actually felt compassion for her. She was a victim just as I was. There were times I raged at my mother for not protecting me and there were times when I felt her pain.

My father escorted me to my room where he made me perform oral sex on him. I had to hate myself for that. Sure, I was a child, but no one would let their father do such unbelievably horrible things to her if she had any guts. I had no guts. I had nothing to sustain me. I was worse than garbage.

I wept then, for the joys of life and joys lost, as Nora Roberts so aptly put it.

Chapter 10

Susan age 12-14

Deep Chronic Wounds

"Emotional wounds with a link to independence come up in situations where someone is too controlling with you. Usually what happens is that someone with power over you, uses that power arbitrarily. But by doing that, they do a lot of damage to your personal feeling of independence"
(exploringyourmind.com)

As I approached my teenage years, I was becoming increasingly confused and anxious. I felt my time was almost up. Somehow I knew if I did not act soon, my father was going to cross the line and rape me. While I always thought sexual molestation was equal to rape, I felt that this final act was better to be avoided.

One must consider my state of mind by this time. I was in extreme fear of my father. I had seen his violence against my mother increasing. On one such occasion, he threw her through the glass door that separated the dining room from the living room in my house. I do realize now how easily she could have died from this act. The glass could have cut through an artery or the landing on her back or head could have injured her severely. He also threw her out of the house on one bitter, cold winter night. My mother only wore a thin cotton night shirt at the time plus she was barefoot. The temperature outside was well below freezing. In his drunken rage, he locked the door to prevent her from coming back inside again. She knocked on the window in my room, and I let her in. She spent the rest of the night in my room and it took a long time for her to warm up.

When my father was drunk his cruelty reached new heights. I wondered again if he harbored a hatred for females. I do not know enough about his childhood to confirm that suspicion. If one would have asked him he would have definitely denied the very idea. He would have pointed out that he adored women. Did he not have an avalanche of women he had bedded? Be that as it may, he sure as hell did not respect them. He saw the women he bedded as trophies, especially when they were married. He took special pride in sleeping with women who belonged to other men. He even had the audacity to present these women to my mother and made her serve them coffee. She was as fully aware of that fact as I was. While I was outraged, my mother took this insult with stoic nonchalance. I assume she was numb by now. As long as she had her prayers and not too many beatings, she could take anything.

I do believe that my father craved complete control over my mother and me. While we were both scared to death of him, he could never claim perfect rule. I do not think it is altogether possible to dominate another human being completely. And anything but complete will not do for narcissists. But schizophrenia has components that are impenetrable. You see, my father and narcissists in general have this notion that their image has to be perfect. Especially in the eyes of others. And my mother was hilarious in downsizing that image.

She would use a wheelbarrow to carry her purchases, parading all over town. I still get the giggles thinking about that. When she got home, my father would roar at the top of his voice at her, how she had put shame on him. She also had the habit of cleaning the garden fence in pouring rain, which would send my father in a towering rage just because the neighbors would be talking.

I was not fully controlled by him either. If I was, I would not have gone through with my plan to find a guy to take my virginity before he did. I would not have run away without his permission when I felt I could not take it any longer. And I would have not stolen money from his wallet when I wanted an ice cream. I felt no guilt; he owed me that much at least.

However, I clearly feared him so very much. I hated being afraid all the time. I was so tired of being afraid. As I previously said, I feared fear more than anything. It gave me stomach cramps. I felt revulsion towards my father, a terrible nausea that caused me bouts of vomiting. I had to deal with panic attacks and a weight on my heart so heavy that I felt physical pain at the pressure. I also had a deep tension that was manifested inside of me since very early childhood and to this day I fight the remnants of it.

If I felt this way, I wonder how my mother felt. I knew she was in a state of constant exhaustion. Plus, the physical pain from the beatings, not to mention the mental strain. Writing this book, I have a whole new appreciation for her.

It is important to note that in my teenage years, I had issues as high as Mount Everest. I was as insecure as one could get. I was a mediocre student in school and terrified to speak up in class. I was so afraid of humiliation and worthlessness. I recently found out that I have a condition called directional dyslexia. If I had known that as a child, it would have explained why I had such trouble remembering driving directions or my troubles with geometry. My father used this weakness whenever he was displeased with me, and reminded me constantly how stupid I was. Report card time was pure agony for me. I actually had decent grades, save for mathematics. He ignored all my good subjects though and focused on the one that I barely passed.

If that was not enough, I had an identity crisis as well. I could not figure myself out. Who was I? For sure I wasn't a brave girl in my estimation. No one in their right mind would let their father abuse them the way I did. At school I tried to fit in with the cool kids, but was not very successful. I just wasn't cool. They sensed that I was a fake. Even though boys thought me naïve and not very bright, they did find me pretty. This did not particularly cheer me. I felt I was in a freefall. I did not belong at school and I belonged even less at home. My father too had commented on my beauty, stating that I would be a woman soon. It felt like a death sentence to me. It meant my time was up; he would rape me soon. I felt I was on a constant tightrope. I honestly was tired of the constant pressure and even more tired of always fighting. I seemed to be in an endless combat for my very existence. With all the other problems I had, there was now a depression on top of it.

Narcissists, such as my father, have no idea what they are doing to their children's mind. One of the most profound feelings I had growing up that followed me deep into adulthood was the fear of mistakes. I positively felt suicidal when I made any mistake. Let's say for example I slammed the door by mistake. I would get such a yelling and insulting browbeating from my father that I seriously considered killing myself. His message was that any mistake was unforgivable, the little ones as well as the big ones. The horrible crushing fear of mistakes had stayed with me until recently. I have finally learned that it was not the end of the world to make mistakes. In fact, making them was totally human and totally forgivable. This concept of being kind to myself was completely new to me. It did not come easy to me either. It took and still takes considerable practice. The phrase "love yourself" was close to impossible for me. It didn't make sense to me. Once I understood it, it filled me with regret. I realize now that I could have been a better mother had I practiced self-love. In my defense, I have tried my very best with motherhood, but it would have helped to have that knowledge. I would have tried anything to be a good mother, including the foreign concept of self-love, had I known about it.

Self-love was a really difficult thing for me to grasp. This makes sense since self-hate was so ingrained in my being. Rethinking something that sits so deep in one's soul is not easy but it is possible. To all the people out there who practice self-hate, be kind and patient with yourself. It will open up a flood of forgiveness and all the poison that flowed in your veins will leave your body. It will give you such freedom and joy. Do it not for the person who wronged you, but for yourself. So, you can leave the bondage of bitterness. Don't clutch the chains that bind you. Forgive yourself, so you can give unconditional and unrestricted love to those who mean the most to you.

And now that I have done my sermon on that matter, back to my story. I had to find a dude who would take my virginity. God, this was crazy. I could not help but dissolving into giggles every time I thought about it. I pictured myself confronting a poor chap who was nursing his beer.

"Hello, my dear, would you mind deflowering me?"

The poor man would choke on his drink and spit out, "What?"

At this point, the thinking process always stopped because fits of laughter were coming to my surface. The whole thing was silly. I could easily forget the seriousness and the desperation behind the plan. It also occurred to me that the whole idea was immoral. As soon as the thought entered my head, I dismissed it. My whole life was immoral, what harm could one more indecent scheme do?

I did not have the luxury of time and nobility. I had to put my plan into action and soon. I had stolen enough money from my father's wallet for a train ticket, some drinks, and some food at the fair. I found it ironic that my father was indirectly sponsoring me for ridding myself from the burden of being a virgin.

Then Saturday finally came. I left the house early before my father was up and had any chance of interrogating me. I wore a short denim skirt and an army shirt knotted at the waist, barring my midriff. High topped sneakers completed my outfit. I thought I was fully equipped for my mission. I was fourteen, but I thought I could pass easily for sixteen. It occurred to me that the whole deal of picking out a stranger and manipulating into sleeping with me was as unromantic as a business proposal. I justified the action in my mind. This was a move of desperation and desperation always warranted a little craziness.

The knowledge I had acquired so far was that sex was a power game. It was all about manipulation and trickery. My plan proved it, didn't it? I was baiting a guy to sleep with me, not because I had any romantic notion, but because I wanted to avoid my father.

I was using deceit to get this done. I made myself look older because I thought sixteen sounded a lot better than fourteen when your aim was to get a guy into bed with you. By the way, it never occurred to me that this might be illegal. I am not even sure about the consensual sex laws in Germany at this time. And so, I went off on my trip to sex and sin. I was in no way skilled in the art of flirting. Well, I would have to wing it; that was all.

I arrived at the fairgrounds, bought myself a coke and cotton candy, and eyed the unsuspecting males that were present. One was sitting at the bar, contemplating his beer and looking gloomily at the bar tender. He was approximately twenty-five years old. I marked him as a potential candidate. Then there was Mr. Cool by the bumper cars, smoking a cigarette in perfect James Dean mode. There were plenty of other males, but I dismissed all of them for one reason or another. I had to make a choice between the two of them. I decided to go for the loner at the bar. He seemed the easier target.

Jesus H. Roosevelt Christ, how the hell was I going to pull this off? Well, I thought, taking a seat next to him at the bar might be a good start. I did just that and ordered another coke. As much as I wished for something stronger, I had to be careful. Underage drinking was not very strict in Germany, but one never knew which bar tenders were sticklers for that.

The bartender was about to charge me for the coke when my elected victim told him to put it on his tab. Well! This was better than I had expected.

"Thank you," I said. I sent him what I thought was a dazzling smile.

"You are welcome little lady," was his reply. And then, "What's your name?"

I had decided to use a fake name for this operation.

"Diana, and yours?"

"My name is Andy," he replied. "And what is a young lady such as yourself doing here all

by herself?"

I thought, my dear boy, if I told you the truth about that you would be shocked. Instead I took a sip of my coke and said, "Just having some fun."

"Well that is a good reason. Want to dance?"

The band was playing a slow Kenny Roger's song. I thought this was a good chance to get in touch, so to speak. I actually did not like dancing since my grandfather's birthday. This was different however. I had to establish some intimacy and what was better than a dance?

I smiled and said, "Yes, I would love to."

He put an arm around my waist. It didn't feel half bad. It was a lot better than my father's unwanted touches. I began to sway in rhythm with the music and did what I seldom do, I relaxed.

My mind, as always in situations that were utterly crazy, turned to humor. I decided that hunting for some poor dude who would do me the honor of deflowering me was hilarious. And now this poor devil that I picked out was doomed. We had more drinks. All non-alcoholic for me and alcoholic for Andy. He was getting a buzz and I thought that was good. It would be easier to convince him of my purpose if he was in an intoxicated state. I wished I was as well.

In the end, it was he who asked me if I wanted to have a drink at his house. I was giddy with excitement. I had him now. I would lose my virginity and it would take the pressure off me, wondering when my father would force me.

At Andy's house, he offered me a drink and I was happy that I could now ask for a beer. That would certainly help me to be more at ease. As much as I wanted to get this over with, I was scared of it as well. We sat on his couch. After I had my third beer and a slight buzz myself, I felt Andy kissing me. I had been kissed before, by a class mate and by my father, and neither one of them felt good. Andy's technique did not really do the trick either. However, I thought I'd try a little experimenting of my own on him. I returned the kiss and let my tongue play in his mouth. Much to my shock, it turned him on big time. It did something for myself as well. It was a strange feeling of power being capable of exciting a stranger.

Andy breathed heavily and untied the knot of my blouse. He ran his hands over my breasts and then I felt his hand under my skirt. All of a sudden, he was in a hurry. He pulled my panties down and hastily got rid of his pants. I stopped him just in time to put a condom on. No way was I getting pregnant. He entered me and I froze in shock at the pain. My god, did that hurt. I wanted to shout at him to stop but I had somehow lost my voice. Mercifully, the whole thing was over in under a minute.

I lay on the floor of his living room, dazed and so very sore. It felt like a knife had gone through my center. There was a little blood on the floor, but that was the least of my worries now. So, I had gone through with my plan and was no longer a virgin. I had the pain as evidence. So, this is what sex was all about? God alone knew why females would want to go through that on their own free will. This was absolutely no fun.

It was at least a comfort knowing that I had prevented my father from doing it to me. I felt in my heart that I had made the right decision by preventing him from being the first man inside of me. It was better, much better, to have a stranger doing this painful thing.

I was getting dressed and Andy was watching me. He apologized for having hurt me. He said he wished he could have controlled himself better and done it more slowly. I was horrified to have the whole thing analyzed at all and told him it had been fine. When I was at the door, Andy asked me for my phone number. I gave him a fake number. I had no desire to ever see him again. Not because I was mad at him. I wasn't. It was just my way of protecting him.

When I got home my father started to question me immediately. Where had I been? And with whom? Had I been whoring around? I was really in no mood to answer these questions. I was sore in my center and wanted nothing more than a shower and some sleep.

I got lucky for once. My father's co-worker called and he was called in for an extra shift. I was saved for the moment and got my wish for a shower and sleep. I hated his lust and I hated my helplessness and my fear of him.

My father raped me a week later. When he found out that I was not a virgin, he was furious. He wanted to know the man of the man who taken his property. I was so glad that I did not even know his last name. For once, I was proud of myself of being bold enough to deny my father. He had used a condom and thank god for small mercies.

I have always hated my helplessness and my fear of him, but just this once, I had done what I felt was right. I had refused him something. I felt wonderfully exalted. It would not last. I would pay dearly for my insubordination.

In the meantime, my practicality had not left me. I was resigned to the fact that he would rape me often now, but I would tell myself that this horror would pass eventually. Besides, the rapes were over much quicker than the molestation and that was a relief. I had arrived at the point where I was thinking the faster those episodes were over, the better.

What I did not know was that my father's next scheme would take me to a new low. I honestly thought things could not get any worse, but I was wrong about that. He would take me to the brink of ending everything, and I am still marveling how I survived it. The following weekend, he took me on a train trip again. I never enjoyed these outings because they implied forced sex. And to be honest, I did not like the company of my father. The constant tension was killing me. I was always waiting for the next blow. Sure enough, he had plotted a revenge on me. He took me to a pub inside a train station. Whatever came next, I thought, at least I would have a drink first.

He left me at the bar and came back with two strange men. While sipping my beer I found out they were Turkish guest workers. I thought my father had wanted some company, naturally someone he deemed lower than him so he could feel superior. Well, that was good, I thought. He would pay less attention to me, if only for a moment.

He gestured with his hands to them since they did not speak German very well and I did not pay attention. After about thirty minutes of this, he told me to get up and led me to the men's bathroom. I was surprised but not yet alarmed.

Then the nightmare came full circle. He watched those men rape me without a condom. I felt my life was over. I had sunk too low. This, I could not overcome. I was nothing. Completely worthless. This knowledge, which was the message all through my childhood, made me unbearably sad. I decided this was too much. I would end my life. I had earned that right. And because no condom was used, maybe I had contracted HIV anyway. That would only add to my shame. I felt I had earned the right to get out of this life once and for all.

When I got home that horrible night, I snuck into my grandmother's unit. All was quiet and they had already gone to sleep. I slipped into the bathroom and extracted a bottle of my grandmother's sleeping pills. I grabbed them and went back into my room. Once there, I poured a glass of water and was about to swallow the contents of the bottle. It would be such a relief to end it all. I would not have to deal with HIV or a pregnancy. Both were possibilities I was so afraid to face. I would not have to deal with the terrible emotional pain of the whole thing. I would be free and at peace. It was so tempting to end it all. There was so much promise of contentment in that notion.

I was ready. I looked at the pills and they were so tempting. They promised eternal sleep and no pain any longer. I wanted to take them, I really wanted to. But then a thought came to me. I could not do it. I could not hurt my brother that way. It would hurt him; I was sure of it. And I loved him. I cannot hurt those I love. Even in my deepest desperation, love was stronger than the pain. Imagining hurting my brother whom I loved so deeply, I could not go through with it. I also realized this would burden him and he may even blame himself. No, I could not inflict that torture on him. I would rather face this hell on earth four more years.

I had a yeast infection after the night that crushed my spirit. I mistook the symptoms for HIV. I thought, I will die after all but not by my own hand. God will take care of it this time. The burning of my vagina was so bad that I used snow to ease it. No way I could tell anyone of my shame. In the end, a friend gave me her vaginal cream and the yeast infection went away. I would have to go on living.

I still hurt mentally and emotionally, but hope is a great thing. It makes things easier to take, even the terrible things. As Martin Luther King said it so well, "We must accept finite disappointment, but never lose infinite hope."

The day would come when I could leave. At least now I knew that I did not have HIV. I would just have to pray that I would not be pregnant and that I could get past these next four years. And how exactly would I survive that? I was not sure; I only knew that I would somehow. The day I turned eighteen I would leave this house, even if I had to live on the street.

There were times when I could not stand the torture any longer. I would run away and slept on park benches to escape the pressure in my house. On one such occasion, I bought a train ticket to Frankfurt. I did not know a soul in that town. I had decided to sleep on a bench near a bus stop when it began to rain. In a few minutes I was soaked. It was beginning to get dark and I resigned myself to a sleepless night. Suddenly a resident next to the bus stop opened his window.

He said, "Child, come on in out of the wet. I will make you a meal and you can take a shower. It is dangerous for you to spend the night on that bench."

I was told not to trust strangers, but hell, I had learned I could not even trust my family. I took a chance and followed him into his house. Once inside, I noticed artifacts from all over the world. Pictures of boats were hanging on the walls and his place was filled with antique vases.

My benefactor showed me his bathroom and offered me a hot shower. He said there were fresh towels and an unopened package with new pajamas I could use. When I entered the kitchen, he had a bowl of hot soup waiting for me and a slice of fresh bread. I ate and he entertained me with stories of his adventures from all over the world. He had been a captain on a cruise ship and his supply of tales seemed endless. I enjoyed them all.

After supper he led me to a couch where he had set up a bed for me. The rain was still pounding on the roof when I went off to sleep, my faith in humanity restored. There was kindness in this world after all and I felt for once, all would be alright in the end.

The next day was Saturday and I had a fine time with Captain Mueller. He made breakfast and I did the dishes. It was the least I could do to thank him for his kindness. We took a walk in the woods and it was peaceful. Back at his house we watched TV. We ate the meals together in companionship and harmony. I wished I could have stayed with him forever.

I knew it was a pipe dream. I had to go back to the house of horror. Monday was a school day. If my father had to call a search party, there would be hell for me to pay. He would already be pissed that I had run away again. I will never forget Captain Mueller as long as I lived. Unexpected kindness always warmed me and I was so grateful to him for bringing hope back into my life.

Chapter 11

Susan 16-17

"On the brink of the abyss, if you look into the abyss, the abyss stares back at you" (Friedrich Nietzsche).

At the age of sixteen, I now focused on a plan to escape my parent's house. I had two more years to go, but I felt hope surging through me. Finally, I saw the light at the end of the tunnel.

One day, my father announced that I would accompany him to the state capital. Oh well, I thought, another one of those horrible trips with hotel rooms and me performing sexual acts. I took comfort in the fact that my eighteenth birthday would come in the not too far future.

This trip was slightly different. My father had actually arranged for me to have an audition in pornographic movies. He had not mentioned this to me. So, I sat on the train mentally preparing myself for what I considered the usual fair.

Upon arrival in the city, he first took me to the bar. I think that was calculated. It was better for that purpose he had in mind if I was not totally sober. I was less stiff and shy when somewhat intoxicated. I was nearly 17 by now and no bar in Germany would ask me for an ID. My father also saw that I was no longer so frightened at his ventures, rather, I had become apathetic. This was not good for his purposes. This spiritless disposition took away from his pleasure and his business plans, if he had any for me. So, he made this rule that I should be not sober when on one of his missions. This was fine with me because I found it much easier to endure these horror trips in a drunken state. I thought, whatever his purpose was for this trip, at least I was properly drunk. I had three whiskeys on the rocks and my head was spinning.

When we arrived at the porn studio, I did not recognize it as such. I saw the cameras and the different rooms and wondered what on earth this was. The director gave us a brief tour and asked me about my previous experiences in this brand of film making. I informed him, in a highly intoxicated state, that I had all kinds of experience when it came to sex but had never been on film. He looked at me in a condescending way and smiled.

He said, "My darling, I am sure you will be marvelous. Before we start making a screen test, all of our debutants have to take a test of a different kind... to examine their skills so to speak."

In my ignorance I actually thought he wanted to test me in mathematics. Whenever I heard the word test, I automatically associated it with algebra and geometry. Those were my worst subjects in school. I will flunk, I thought. Well good, I do not want to be in porn movies anyway. When I informed him that I "sucked" at math, he smiled at me again.

"My dear, it isn't that kind of a test," he sat down on a chair and asked me to kneel before him. "I want you perform a blow job on me."

I was obediently going into the desired position when nausea took hold of me. I dashed to the bathroom. My body was not used to the whiskey and I vomited until green bile came out of my mouth. Even though I had vomited, the alcohol was still in my blood and the high remained. I rinsed my mouth out with the mouth wash that was always part of my purse's inventory. When I returned to the director, he asked me if I was up to the job now.

Still intoxicated, I was quite flippant. I said, "Sure, no worries."

I was done in less than a minute. My father was very proud of me. That was a fact that almost made me vomit again. It made me think that I was not a person to him. I was a tool at best. Not someone who had feelings and thoughts. I was an object that he could use as he saw fit. The sadness that was so much a part of me during that time, threatened to overpower me. The emotional pain made my eyes sting and so I excused myself to the bathroom once more.

We left the building and my father felt he needed to have a talk with me. He began by telling me I had tested very well and we would definitely be back here when I was eighteen.

Then he looked at me sharply and said, "You did extremely well, but we must limit your alcohol intake. I will be more watchful on what you order and on how much."

Ha, I thought with glee, you will not control me at all anymore once I am eighteen! I am about to make my exit from your control by that time once and for all.

Chapter 12

Susan age 17

"Hope" is the thing with feathers-

that perches the soul-

And sings a tune without the words-

And never stops-at all-

(Emily Dickinson)

At seventeen, I was preoccupied with various plans on how to move out the very next year. This prospect kept me so busy that I endured my father's various abuses with stoic apathy. I was now really close to freedom and focused on planning my escape. One more year and I was home free. I racked my brain how I was going to accomplish this. There had to be a way.

During that time, I worked in the packing department of a meat company. As I sat in the cafeteria eating my lunch, I looked at the people around me. My view fell on table where a single man sat. He was a black man, handsome, and I guessed his age to be about in his early thirties. I studied him intently and decided he was the one. He fulfilled all my requirements. He was not German, that was the most important. I did not trust German men anymore. I was convinced he had an apartment I could move in with him once I turned eighteen. I would not be a burden to him. After all, I had a job, too.

I pondered the problem of how I could convince him to let me move in with him. He was a man and would probably see me as a little girl who had lost her mind. Well, I had some advantages, too. I was pretty and young. I was also, for better or worse, rather mature due to the life that I had led so far.

But first things first. How on earth was I going to approach this man? Sure, I had sexual experience of the worst kind, but I had no experience on seducing a man. Other than my attempt with Andy, who had taken my virginity, I was an amateur. And that did not even count. There was much more at stake this time. I was determined to get this man to let me move in with him. I had roughly a year to accomplish that. He was not an easy man to convince, but I was desperate.

Being fluent in the art of seduction might have helped in this case, but I was not very good at artificial allurement. I said to myself, good or not, you want to get out of the house of maniacs; therefore, you have to do your best in tempting this poor man. I laughed at myself inwardly. Dear god, I found myself constantly in weird situations. And now for it.

I grabbed my lunch tray; I remember the meal was meatloaf, mashed potatoes with peas, and rice pudding for dessert. I marched resolutely in the direction where my victim was unsuspectingly reading the newspaper and simultaneously eating his lunch. When I reached him, I asked politely if it was okay if I shared his table. I spoke English, which seemed to amuse him.

"Well sure little girl," he said with some surprise.

I sat down and started to eat my lunch. I waited for him to start a conversation. I found out that he wouldn't. Great, I thought, he is not making this easy on me. I was still desperately searching for a topic of conversation when my mind shifted. Something came out of my mouth that I had not planned to say.

"Do you have a girlfriend?" I asked. As soon as I had said it, I regretted the question.

He raised his eyebrows and looked at me thoughtfully.

Finally, he said, "What a leading question, my dear."

My first thought was, I blew it. No way he will be interested in me after this question. I made the fatal mistake of coming on to him. My insecurity took over and with it came shame. My father's words came to my mind: "You are no prize for any man." According to him, I had no skills, was too stupid to even pass a driver license test, did not cook very well, and only had a lowly high school diploma. I was only good at one thing, he had said with sarcasm dripping from his voice, and that was for feeding his needs. But rest assured I would not need A's in mathematics for that. For some reason this assessment wounded me worse than most of his other abuses and insults. Every mistake I made was magnified. The pain of my incompetence hurt me deep in my soul. It would haunt me for the rest of my life. I was ready to give up, but for once I could not bring myself to quit so easily. I had to win over this man. My very existence was at stake. I took a deep breath and apologized.

"I did not mean to offend you. I was just curious," I said with a nervous laugh.

I think he felt my discomfort and decided to give me a break and answer my question.

"No, I do not have a girlfriend at this time. Do you want to volunteer?"

There it was, the very question. I knew he was teasing me but this was the perfect opportunity to lay the cards on the table. I took in another deep breath and answered truthfully.

"Yes, I would," I said simply as I looked straight into his eyes.

He did not think that funny and his expression became very serious.

"My dear, I do not want to be your boyfriend; I can definitely live without a complication like that."

"Why not?" I asked. I was crushed. I tried to hide my panic. I could not have lost the game already, I thought desperately.

"My dear, you cannot seriously ask that question. If we dated it would create a scandal of epic proportions in this town. Think of your parents! They would have a fit. What would your father think?"

I scowled, and thought, my father does not want me to date anyone. He is a sick asshole and I wish I would never see him again in my life! He is the very cause of my sitting here trying to get a date with you! Those were my thoughts. I dared not voice them.

Instead I said, "Never mind what my father thinks. Would you go out with me?"

There. I said it. I waited for his answer.

He looked at me with an annoyed expression on his face. Then he asked, "And how the hell can I say no to that?"

I grinned and said, "What is your name?"

He smiled too, "I was wondering when you would ask me that. My name is Malek."

"I am…" I began to say.

He interrupted me, "I know your name."

"You do?" I asked with astonishment.

"Yes, I have noticed you. I referred to you in my mind as the very pretty girl from the packing department. I asked my supervisor and he told me your name is Susan."

Being called pretty always embarrassing me somehow. It is a strange thing in a way. I always secretly thought my physical attributes were responsible for the sexual abuse I had endured. On the other hand, I knew that looks played a part in winning over men to your side. It was easier to persuade men when you were considered pretty.

I myself was in conflict almost every time I looked in the mirror. I liked my appearance, but I hated my character. I wasn't a hero. I had let my father abuse and rape me, I had not protected my mother from beatings of her husband, and I had not stood up for myself. Worst of all, I was scared most of the time. These thoughts flooded through my mind and I had to push them out quickly. This was no time for self-reflection. Focus, I said firmly to myself. You need a date with Malek and right now that is all that matters. At this moment the buzzer rang and our lunch break was over.

We looked at each other and then Malek said, "Let's meet again for breakfast at this table. And no, that is not a date."

"Not yet," I replied grinning, "but it is a start!"

It was breakfast time and we met again. After we exchanged pleasantries he said, "This is only a fifteen-minute break and therefore, I want you to listen carefully to what I am saying."

I nodded put my head on my elbows and looked at him expectantly.

"I know you want to go out with me, and trust me I am tempted. You are pretty and young and you have an engaging personality. One seldom finds those three attributes combined in one person. However, there is no way this can work."

I wanted to interrupt but he held out a hand to stop me.

"I know what you want to say. You think race does not matter, age does not matter, and what people will say does not matter. Very admirable principles to be sure, but my girl, you could lose your family."

I had to giggle at this. The irony was just too great. Here I was trying to get away from my family and he was worried about me losing those very ties. I looked at the clock and knew that the break was almost over.

"Let's just meet again for lunch," I said. "And for god's sake let's have a real date soon. These breaks are just not long enough for a conversation."

He gave me an exasperating look and could not help a smile. "Fine," he said, "see you at lunch."

When I went back to my work station, I was surprised to find people staring at me. My first thought was that I forgot to put on my hairnet and hastily pulled it over my head. As I went to my workstation, I found that I had gotten it wrong. My hairnet was not the reason for the stares. People positively started glowering at me.

What the hell was the matter with everyone, I mused. Then, finally it became impossible for them to hold their silence any longer. The dominant female of my team, Millie, spoke up.

"Susan, are you actually thinking of getting involved with a black man?"

I was shocked and outraged. How dare she ask me such an intimate question? Of all the incredible nerve, I thought. It wasn't in my nature to defy my elders but this was going too far. I seethed with anger. It took all my strengths to speak in measured tones.

"My dear Miss Millie," I said, "what a leading question. I am quite sure that is none of your business." My voice, despite my iron control, shook slightly. Partly from daring to be defiant and partly from fury.

Her large bosom heaved at my affront. "You ought to be ashamed," she snarled, "I shall inform your parents of your conduct. The way you speak to me is unacceptable. Not to mention that you are friendly with a black man. I am putting this mildly. God only knows what real intentions you have with this foreigner."

By this time, I was beyond angry. How dare this old crocodile berate me on my relationships? Why couldn't everybody shut up and mind their own business? But that was not to be. The rest of my work group looked at me with a mixture of curiosity and disgust. I took a deep breath and decided to take the bull by the horns.

"Does anybody else have any objection of me being friendly with Malek?" I asked defensively.

Annie, Julia, Gudrun, and Hilda looked at me open mouthed.

Annie pompously said, "You cannot be serious Susan. He is a black man. He has a different culture, different rules. He is from Africa, likely from a tribe. Susan, it would never work. You have no idea how they treat their women. Women are second class citizens in their countries. Aside from all of that, you belong with our boys, the white German boys. You cannot suddenly go against all rules. It is not done."

I listened to that sermon with incredulity. I could hardly believe my ears. She actually had the nerve to say something about how other countries treated their women. Ha, that was a laugh, I thought bitterly. I wish she would take a good look at her surroundings. I was quite sure that she had seen my mother's black eyes before and heard the rumors in town. This was a subject that was only discussed in whispers and out of earshot of my family. Strangely enough, it was my mother who was criticized, not my father. This was the irony of our culture; it put shame on the victim rather than the abuser. Thus, my mother had to live with the physical and emotional pain of being isolated and battered. And now these silly women had the nerve to talk to me, of all people about other cultures and how they treated their women. Well, good luck bringing up that topic with me!

I said firmly, "Look Annie, I am not going to discuss my friendships with you. Think whatever you want, but this is my decision not yours. And that is the end of this discussion. Let's go back to work and see to it that we do not have this talk again."

Annie glared at me and said, "I will talk to your parents about your impudence, mark my words."

Tension-filled hours followed until lunch time. When the bell finally rang, I stepped out of the packing room quickly and practically raced to the cafeteria. I couldn't wait to see Malek and report to him the events that had taken place at my work station. I saw him sitting at his usual table in the cafeteria. I was among the first in the lunch line. I grabbed my tray and went straight to Malek's table. I sat down opposite of him and while we were eating gave him an account of the events that had taken place after breakfast. His reaction to my report stunned me.

He looked at me with a serious expression and asked, "My poor innocent, what did you expect? I tried to explain to you earlier if I date you it is going to be a scandal."

"But it is none of their business!" I exclaimed. "What does skin color matter anyway? It means nothing to me, only that I find black skin beautiful. Not that that matters. As long as a person is kind to me, I do not care if he is black, green, or purple. I measure a man by kindness, for it has been a rarity in my life."

Malek looked at me and I could tell that he suddenly saw me in a different light. There was reluctant respect in his eyes.

He looked at me thoughtfully and said, "Susan, you are one of the very few people I have ever known that has no bigotry in them. That is amazing because I am quite sure that you were not raised that way. In this little town there is no room for a revolution. And yet something or someone has convinced you that skin color does not matter. You are really quite a remarkable person, Susan."

As always, any praise embarrassed me. My view was that there was nothing remarkable about me. I saw myself as incredibly flawed. I wasn't heroic, certainly not smart, and I had no self-confidence. I was no catch to be sure. But if Malek thought I was worthwhile, who was I to object? I needed to move in with him and I had less than a year to do it. Life is very hard when you do not like yourself. And I was so far from it.

From then on, Malek and I spent our breaks together. That was a start, but if we were to live together I needed to get to know him on a more intimate level. Guys did not let a girl live with them if they did not know how they were in bed. I had no illusions about that. Surely, I was not squeamish thinking about that. Not after what I have been through. Deep down I knew that this was not the same as the abuse I was used to. I did this voluntary and not with force. True, there was a purpose behind it, but I was attracted to Malek. I liked him. I liked his mind, his kindness, his brains, and yes, his body.

I wanted a date with him and figured that I had to ask since I was fairly sure he wouldn't. I had the feeling he wanted to go out with me but had deep reservations about it. He feared the whispers and open scorn. I knew there would be some of that, but thought it worth the risk.

I took a deep breath and said, "Malek would you like to go and see a movie on Saturday?"

He closed his eyes and sighed deeply.

"Do I want to do that? Sure, I do. But Susan, everyone is going to have a fit. Starting with the people right here in this cafeteria. Your family will definitely not be happy if I take you out. Come to think of it, I am not even sure my family back in Senegal would be happy if we were dating either."

I looked straight into his eyes and asked the question that was most on my mind, "Malek, what about you? Do you want to date me?"

It was his turn to look into my eyes. Much to my shock he took my hand and held it tenderly.

Then he said, "Of course I want to date you. You are a beautiful girl with a great personality. I know this is not going to end well, but I will take you out this Saturday against my better judgement. I will pick you up at your house on Saturday at 6:00pm."

A strange panic rose inside of me. For all my bravado, I was afraid of Malek picking me up at my house. I feared my mother's disapproval and my father's wrath. In addition to that,

I thought if they saw Malek taking me out it could destroy my plans of moving out at eighteen. If they disapproved, and they most certainly would, I might not escape them as soon as I became of legal age.

Malek must have seen the conflict in my face. He smiled and said, "Susan, you have a lousy poker face. I can read your thoughts plainly on your face. I will make it easy for you. Let's meet at the park. Your parents won't see me and you can save yourself your anxiety. Then I do not have to face my own unease either."

The break was almost over and I quickly agreed.

"Saturday at 6:00 it is," I got up from the table, smiled, and said, "I am delighted."

Malek saw me retreat and said, "Yeah me too."

Saturday could not come soon enough. The days seemed to drag on. Finally, the big day had come. I got up early, ate breakfast, helped my mother straighten up the house, and stayed out of my father's way. This was easy since he left for work at 7:30am. At noon, I had a light lunch and then I watched a movie on tv.

By 4:00, I had butterflies in my belly and it was time to get ready for my date with Malek. First order of business was to take a shower and brush my teeth. Then I had to style my hair; no easy feat since I had an unruly mane that was not easy to tame. In the end I settled for a pony tail that made me look clean and fresh. I applied some light makeup of lipstick, eyeshadow, and blush. The question now was what to wear. Not that I had many choices. In the end I settled for my best pair of form fitting jeans and an army shirt. That was pretty much the uniform for teenagers in Germany at the time. I added some golden hoop earrings and my wrist watch. A denim jacket completed my outfit. I was ready one hour before Malek was due to meet me at the park that was only a five-minute walk away. Nervously I brushed my teeth again and added some light perfume. Finally, it was time to leave. I grabbed my purse containing a handkerchief and my wallet. I did not have keys to my house, so I left the basement door open and my window. It was likely that my father would be home by the time I came back from my date and then it was not advisable to be seen by him.

I arrived at the park with five minutes to spare. Malek was already there and that was a surprise. Was it possible that he was nervous too? If he was, he hid it well.

"Well, Miss Susan, good to see you. You look beautiful," He smiled down at me.

Then he grabbed my hand and said, "Let's go."

As usual, I felt slightly uncomfortable when called me beautiful. I always had the feeling my beauty was fake. How could I be beautiful when I let my father do things to me that were simply wrong and disgusting? I had no real worth if I could not stand up for myself. I had no character. While quite pretty on the outside to some people, I knew I was completely rotten on the inside. I had no dignity, no courage, and no self-confidence. How could I be beautiful?

We walked to the train station and made light conversation. We talked about movies we had seen and music we liked. We reached the station just in time to take the short train ride to the neighboring city that offered a movie theater. We had two hours to kill before the start of the movie and Malek suggested an ice cream parlor. We both ordered a banana split. I happily gobbled up the treat and chatted lightly with Malek.

Suddenly he said, "Do you realize that we are being watched?"

I glanced around. Indeed, there were people staring at us. There was whispering as young and old people observed us disapprovingly. One young man looked at us with the most open hostility. Much to my shock, he approached our table.

"Aren't you ashamed of yourself?" He asked.

I looked at him with incredulity. I was truly perplexed. I thought, I am plenty ashamed of myself, but not for the reason you think.

"I don't see why I should be," I answered evenly.

He looked at me with disgust, gave me the finger, and spat, "Black man's whore."

Malek had not interfered in this exchange so far, but his face was tight. I could tell that he had reached his limit of tolerance.

He looked straight into the stranger's face and said in a dangerously low voice, "What have you just said?"

"You heard me," was the response.

"Yes I did," Malek said. He was about to get up from his chair, but I sent him a pleading look and laid my hand over his.

"Please let's not spoil this day. He is not worth it. Let's just go."

As we left, the young man continued to yell insults at us. For some reason that made me laugh. It was ridiculous really, the bigotry of people. In my mind, they got it all wrong. There was so much injustice in the world, even in my own family, but people chose to focus on something as inconsequential as skin color. To this day, it does not make sense to me.

We finally went to the movie theatre and had a fine time. We ate popcorn and were safe from any dirty looks. We talked more about general things and then took the last train home. I really did not want this day to end. I guess Malek did neither. I had a great time and was dreading the thought of going home. I did not want to run into my father. I did not want to answer questions of where I had been and I did not want to risk being used by my father. I wanted to end this day without tension. I wanted to hold on to the happiness of this day.

I still wonder where I got the courage, but I asked Malek if he could take me back to his apartment. There was a shocked silence and it took a full minute before Malek found his voice.

"Susan, how old are you?"

I wanted to say eighteen, but I found I could not lie about my age to this man who had given me such a beautiful day. Therefore, I answered truthfully.

"I am seventeen," I answered.

He looked at me kindly. "I am glad you are not lying to me," he said softly.

I felt the sexual tension between us and was quite sure he felt it too. There was an undeniable electricity, but there was also hesitation on his part.

He looked at me intently. He said slowly, "Susan, I am not denying wanting you. That would be foolish dishonesty. You are so young, so pretty, and so sweet. I do not want to take advantage of you. If I take you back to my place, I might not be able to resist."

I looked up at his face and kissed him lightly on the lips. Before I could say anything though, he backed me against a nearby tree. He looked at me intently and then he kissed me. Hot and hard, he parted my lips and his tongue invaded my mouth. It was a thrill I had never felt before. I felt myself responding and it took both of our breath away.

Reluctantly Malek let go of my mouth and asked hoarsely, "Do you really want to go to my place?"

"Yes, yes. Let's go," I replied in a shaky voice.

We walked the 45 minutes from the train station to his apartment. I enjoyed the cool night air and neither one of us spoke much. When we at last entered the door to his apartment, I thought I had finally cooled off a bit. The place was sparsely furnished but clean. Malek asked me if I would like a drink. I took off my jacket and Malek handed me a beer. Then he took me into his living room and opened the window. We looked at the stars and drank our beers.

The feeling of his male nearness renewed my feeling of arousal. Malek backed me up to the wall and we kissed again. The heat consumed me. My breath came out uneven and I could not prevent a low moan. His hands slid over my shirt and he slowly opened the buttons. He cupped my breasts and pulled my bra down. He was gentle and in charge at the same time. When he finally entered me, I felt I had come home. I forgot my father and his abuse, my mother's disorder, and the tension of how to explain the next morning that I had failed to come home the whole night.

When I woke the next morning in Malek's apartment, a slight panic bubbled up inside of me. I pushed it aside and we made love again. We then had breakfast. And with the energy of young, new lovers ended up in bed again. Later I suggested a walk and Malek looked at me questionably.

"A walk you say, baby, in broad daylight? Have you forgotten the neighbors? The foundation of this little town is going to shake violently. You really do not understand this, do you? Relations with me will create a scandal of amazing proportions."

I looked crestfallen. I never understood this whole race thing. In my mind, skin color did not matter. My criteria for a relationship was not based on looks at all. I just wanted someone kind and good natured. I had seen so much hate, jealousy, and resentment. I felt if anyone was half decent to me, I would give him the world.

Out loud I said, "Why can't people focus on themselves? Why does it matter if someone is gay or black? Is Jewish or prays to cows? All of that is so irrelevant if they are a good person."

"Oh, my sweet innocent," Malek smiled, "if only the world would see humanity through your eyes it would be a wonderful place. Really, Susan, you surprise me. You have this wonderful world view and I am quite sure you were not raised that way. You are a rare and unique woman."

"Hardly that, my dear. But thank you," I said with slight discomfort once again.

I was just not used to kind, genuine words. I could not shake the feeling that was so ingrained inside of me. I was not worth much. Even though I have gotten much better at giving myself some credit, to this day I am battling this feeling of not being enough.

We did have our walk. People stared with silent disapproval. I will admit as much as it discomforted me, I also found it hilarious. I imagined all the outraged conversations on the dinner tables in my little hometown community. I could not help but giggle at the image.

Then came the time when I had to go home and face my family. "Family" meaning my father, really. As I had expected, he drilled me with questions. He called me a whore for having stayed away all night. I wish I could say that I did not mind much, but the truth was that the tension he instilled in me was terrible. The anxiety was so intense that it almost physically hurt. His jealously was palpable. My feelings of disgust toward him were as bad as my fear of him.

It became very clear to me that the last six months in this house of horrors would be pure hell for me. How could I sleep with Malek and endure the abuse of my father at the same time? Could I tell Malek about my father's abuse? No, that was out of the question. I did not want to jeopardize my relationship with him. After all, he was my ticket to a little freedom. Aside from the fear that my secret would destroy my newfound normalcy with Malek, I could not tell him for another reason. I just could not share my shame with anyone. It would be more than I could bare.

Chapter 13

Out

"If you are trying to achieve, there will be roadblocks. I've had them; everybody has had them. But obstacles don't have to stop you. If you run into a wall, don't turn around and give up. Figure out how to climb it, go through it, or work around it"
(Michael Jordan).

The vicious gossip about my relationship with Malek spread like a wildfire. It reached my parents in no time. My mother was thunderstruck and my father furious. I myself waited for the ugly confrontation with him. I knew it would come and soon. What people thought did not matter one bit to me, but with my father it was a different story. Not that his opinion had any value to me, but the element of fear was so prominent in me. My terror toward him that lived inside of me would never completely leave me until his death. So, when he finally summoned me, I felt an enormous dread.

He ordered me into the living room where he sat on the couch. I stood by the door shaking on the inside and the outside.

He gave me one of his piercing looks and yelled, "So, you've been whoring around, you little bitch? Not only that, you are a black man's whore! Well I can't say I am surprised that you stooped that low. How is fucking him? You are not good at anything but fucking. And if that is what he is after, he's got the grand prize!"

He spoke in an ugly, cutting tone that made me want to drop dead. He was right. I was good for nothing. The shame of his words brought tears to my eyes. My father turned on the TV and that was his signal that I was dismissed. Eyes stinging with tears, I fled the room.

I held on in my parent's house until the day came when I turned eighteen. I had been dreaming of this day for so long. Now it was finally here and I was scared. Get a grip Susan, I berated myself. You leave this house of horrors today, and there is nothing to be scared of. Malek has agreed to take you in and you are finally free.

I had planned to leave my house sneakily, but as luck had it, my father was off work that day. I packed my belongings into two suitcases and a purse. I opened my rooms door carefully in the hopes that my father would not see me. It was not to be. He saw me in the hallway with my hands full.

"Well, well, well," he said with heavy sarcasm, "If it isn't the black man's whore trying to sneak out. Where are you going, girl? On a little whoring vacation with your black man? Not while you are living under my roof."

He stood very close to me and I felt the alcohol on his breath. I tried to get my panic under control. I had come this far and was not going back. Tears wanted to come, but I held them back ruthlessly. Suddenly rage blocked out all fear. I was angry, so very angry. Hate, hot and potent, bubbled up inside of me.

"No," I said in a voice that was as cold as ice, "I am not going on vacation. I am leaving. I am done. I am leaving you and your bullshit."

He slapped me and it nearly knocked me off my feet. I did not care.

"You think your beating up women impresses me, you bastard? It does not. And that is all that you are good for, anyway! I hope you are proud of yourself."

He looked at me incensed. His eyes were full of fury and hate. I had touched a nerve that was deeper than I could have imagined. He struck me again, harder this time. I was beyond caring. I was leaving anyway. Much to my shock, my mother came out of the dining room and took part in the confrontation. It did not surprise me that she took my father's side. She looked at me with accusing eyes.

"I could hear you all the way in the dining room, Susan. How dare you speak to your father that way! You should be ashamed of yourself. Calling your father names. God in his heaven is not happy with you, girl. I am not happy either. I taught you better than that. Have you no shame? As for you moving in with a black man, Susan, that is not done. I do not know where you get these ideas. It is not something I taught you, surely. Such relationships never work out. Like must marry like and that is that."

She paused at that moment in her speech and I thought it was time for me to put a word in. First came a genuine hearty laugh, however. It took a while until my giggles subsided. It amazed me that my laugh had no bitterness behind it. At last, I had composed myself enough to speak my piece.

"My dear Mama," I began, "My very dear Mama. It amuses me that you of all people see yourself as qualified to give me advice on relationships. What was it? Like must marry like? Well, this is the case in your marriage, right? And did it work? I think not. As a matter of fact, you and your husband's matrimony is the worst union I have ever seen. So, do yourself a favor and hold your tongue when it comes to my choices of men."

Suddenly my father screamed, "Out! You are not my daughter anymore. Get out! Do not come back. You will be gone, you hear? You will lose all ties to this family. You will lose your brother and your mother."

At my father's words a bitter laugh welled up in me. I answered in a calm voice that seemed to not be my own.

"My mother? You think I will lose my mother? You cannot be serious. Thanks to you, I lost her years ago. And Mark? I think you are mistaken there. He is not under your control as much as you think. And he will be eighteen next year. I am not afraid of losing him because I won't. And as far as your words go, that I am not your daughter anymore, I shall be delighted! It is a real relief, being disowned that way! The way I see it, this is a true honor."

His face became contorted with rage as he screamed once again, "Get out! Get out and never come back! You have no honor and no shame."

Oh this was rich, I thought. He is talking to me about honor and shame. He was certainly right about me having no honor. But shame was different. Thanks to him, I had enough of that for several lifetimes of that. I would never get over the shame he put on me, I thought miserably. I should say at this point in the recollections of my youth, that the element of shame is a battle I fight to this day. And on that note, I left the house, leaving my father's ranting and raving behind me.

Now that I was out of the house, I made my way over to Malek's apartment. We both took the day off from work so I could settle in. He met me at the bus stop and took my suitcases. There weren't very many people on the bus, but the few that were gave us evil stares. I could not help myself; I had to laugh. Seeing the faces of the old ladies full of disapproval was quite funny to me. It occurred to me that the whole affair was a tempest in the tea pot. Malek looked at me and despite himself, he had to grin too.

We got out after a short ride and walked the few steps to Malek's apartment. People eyed us with open hostility, showed us the finger, whispered, and insulted us. I would and could not take this seriously. I had seen too much and been through too much to let that intimidate me. All it did was tickle my sense of humor. It must have been contagious, for Malek began to see it my way.

When we were safely inside Malek's place, I began to unpack. I felt elated. We made our plans and had agreed that we would take turns cooking. Malek often cooked food Senegalese style and I really liked it. Despite being only eighteen years old, I knew there would be disagreements and difficulties eventually. But I was convinced it could all be worked out.

It did all work out. I had no experiences in natural relationships but I learned quickly. I was so grateful to Malek, that I had no desire to be bitchy. Bitchiness has never been one of my natural gifts. Therefore, Malek and I had a very harmonious relationship. We both worked, shared grocery expenses, and shared the modest rent. Plus, we had great sex. This was a revelation to me. Sex for fun without force. It was wonderful and it was hot. At times it solved conflicts and it was never dull. Spending quite a few hours in the bedroom and other rooms in that little apartment was delightful. Malek was a great lover. He was confident, sensitive, and he knew how to play me. I was adventurous beyond my own belief. I tried things, got rid of my insecurity in that area, and found sex a wild field of delights.

I did not tell Malek about my father's abuse or about my upbringing. He sensed it though. He mentioned several times that something did not add up with me. I was, in his opinion, such a child and such an adult rolled into one. That kind of personality, he said, could only come from hardship. I was full of contradictions, was how he put it. Very naïve and at the same time highly logical, full of sadness and full of humor at the same time. There was one constant in me that did not change, he said. He said I was always fascinating. As always, such praise frightened me. I knew I was damaged goods. I had issues and had no idea on earth how to fix them.

I had moved out now, but I still feared my father. This was a fact that was so disappointing to me. When I made a mistake of any kind, I felt suicidal. My inner judge was such a tyrant and he had the voice of my father. While I had post traumatic issues, I had many happy days, too. I was often very grateful for life. These were conflicts that lived inside of me. The beauty of nature and the horrible feeling that I was not worthy in any way. I see now that I was often depressed, but did not know how to put it in words. I felt guilty about being depressed. There was so much beauty around me, how could I be so ungrateful?

Love was another matter that confused me. Malek spoke of it and told me he loved me. I loved him, but how could he love me? I was the scum of the earth; but he did not know that because I had not told him. In my mind, it was enough if I loved him. No need for him to love me back. It was actually better if he did not. Then I would not feel so much pressure to live up to that. This would become a lifelong pattern with me. To me it was always enough if I loved people. No need to love me back. I did not love myself, so why would anyone love me? It was the biggest challenge of my life: to love and be kind to myself. Later I would learn and it made me incredibly sad that I blocked myself from loving anyone fully. I loved my children with all my being, but I realize now I could have added more substance to that love had I loved myself. It makes me incredibly sad to think that I have withheld love from them. I had such walls around my heart. I never realized that until my current husband pointed that out to me.

In many ways I was a lost soul. I never had structure or a safety net. I always had a feeling of abandonment. I often longed for parents in my childhood years and deep into my adult life. I often felt that a part of my soul was missing and I never quite got that part back. That said, I had many blessings in my life as well. I would eventually be the mother of two beautiful children and they are my pride and my joy. I have entertained the idea of suicide many times in my life, mainly when I had the feeling that I made an unforgivable mistake. I could never act on that thought, however, only because I knew it would hurt the people I love. I just could not cause someone I loved pain. I would rather live with deep depression. It is said that people who cannot love themselves cannot love others. I think that is only partly true. I love the people who are good to me so very much. And I am happy to say, I am finally kinder to myself. I am beginning to love myself as well. It is not an easy process to me.

But back to my eighteenth year and my life with Malek. I was actually happy. Happy and so very grateful. I drowned the slight guilt of using him to get away from my parents. I would repay my debt to him by being very sweet. It was easy because he was kind to me. I always felt, and do in many ways to this day, that I owe people who are kind to me.

Life with Malek was fun. True, the population of the town still had their bigotry and prejudices but I did not care. And neither did Malek. We had both decided to ignore people's opinions on our relationship. All would have been well had it not been for the fact that my father had started to stalk me.

The first time I saw him after my unceremonious exit from my parents' house was in the hallway of Malek's apartment house. I was on duty to clean the stairs in the hallway when he suddenly showed up behind me. This gave me quite a start. He looked down at me with ill-concealed contempt.

"Playing the cleaning lady while whoring with a black man?" he snarled.

At that moment the old lady who lived next door to Malek's apartment entered the hallway. She stopped and looked at the exchange with gleeful curiosity. I knew in no uncertain terms that she was not in favor of my union with Malek.

I looked at my father and then back at the neighbor. My heart was beating hard with anxiety. Why was I always so scared to speak my mind? I was scared to answer my father's question. My brain ordered me not to be a coward for once. I took a deep breath.

"I do not see why this is any of your business," I said tightly and was furious that my voice shook.

"You little slut, you have dishonored your whole family."

I knew he wanted to say more, but he could not risk it in front of the neighbor lady. His response did not bother me as such, it was just that my fear of him was so great. If only I could get rid of that fear. It paralyzed me! It degraded me! It diminished me! I had moved out, but I was not free from my father's grip. There was no escaping the fact that he still terrified me. And as long as that was the case, I was tied to him by that panic. I wondered, and not for the first time, if he had broken me beyond repair. That the wounds and the fear sat too deep. I took comfort in the fact that it was still too early to tell. I had just escaped my house of horrors. I had to give it time.

That night my father called me on the house phone. I picked up the receiver and when I heard his voice I froze. Distress immediately took hold of me. Why couldn't he leave me in peace? How did he even get this number? Well, that was easy enough. I answered the question myself. I was living with Malek. He was listed in the phone book. He knew his address, obviously.

The question was, could I live with this stalking? The obscene phone calls? Was my moving out from my parent's house to Malek's apartment far enough? Only time would answer this question.

Chapter 14

The Immoral Choice

"When a man has been denied the right to live the life he believes in, he has no choice but to become an outlaw" (Nelson Mandela)

My life was still uncertain and full of anxiety. Sure, I had moved out of my parent's house. I had some distance between my father and me, but I had not taken him out of my system. In my naïve eighteen-year-old mind, I had actually reasoned that when I moved out of that house of horrors my spirit would be free. I would find out in the course of my life that the poison in my brain was spreading through other parts of my body and would be very hard to remove. It would take a lifetime of cleansing to wash out all the toxins.

At age of eighteen, however, I thought the simple formula of my removal from the control freak would be enough. Of course, it was an improvement but it did not really free me. I found out a few truths about myself. First, I did not hate men. I liked them just fine as long as they were not German. Second, I did like sex when it was not forced. Third, I could be a good companion and a worthwhile partner.

Was I in love with Malek? I am honestly not sure. I had such walls around heart that without being fully aware of it. I let no one come close enough to cause me heartbreak. I was very grateful to him. That in my mind was equal to love. Later I would find out it is not the same. At the time, if someone would have asked me what I was looking for I would have most likely answered peace.

With so many unresolved issues inside of me, I was not likely going to find it soon. I felt that something was broken inside of me. I was desperately looking for the missing pieces without fully knowing what those pieces actually looked like. If you cannot really identify what is missing, it is hard to fill. Therefore, I felt a void and I did not know how to address it. This was frustrating.

It did not help that I often ran into my father. I lived in a small town and I saw him at the train station where he worked, when I bought tickets to nearby towns, in shops or at the post office, and certainly at community fairs. It was always very uncomfortable and brought terror to my heart. This disappointed me greatly. Why wasn't I growing up? Why wasn't I standing up for myself? Why couldn't I find my dignity?

My life with Malek was harmonious and I began to relax around him. We had some disagreements about minor things like what to watch on TV or which party to attend. His friends became mine since mine had abandoned me. It did not bother me much.

Malek had a slight jealous streak that sit not too well with me. He accused me of flirting with his friends and this caused some arguments. I ended up apologizing for something I had not done. Since I felt I owed him for letting me live with him, I let it go.

My father's harassment became a real concern for me. It produced a restlessness inside of me that I could not shake. I wanted to move. Move further away from my father's reach. I wanted to run. The question was where to? And that meant leaving Malek. How to tell him? It felt to me I was always in trouble. Always running from myself.

The urge to flee was so great that I began to make plans. Where to was the first question. Frankfurt came to my mind instantly. How would I support myself? I would have to find a job in a supermarket or in a factory. I would have to find a place that I could afford. If I had trouble doing that in a small town, how on earth would I do it in Frankfurt? How would I break the news to Malek that I wanted to leave him to move into another town? So many questions and no real answers.

I decided the problem with telling Malek could be put off since I had to find out if the move was even possible. First, I acquired a local Frankfurt newspaper. I began to check out apartments and was horrified at how expensive they were. Then I looked at jobs. They paid a little more than in my hometown, but not enough for me to afford a place on my own.

Well, what I needed was a roommate. I began to scan the advertisements. There were plenty of those. Females seemed safer, so I picked up the phone and got in contact with several ladies who were looking for someone to share their rent. If I managed to get a cashier's job in a supermarket and move in with a roommate, I was in business. I called a few of the job offers and was encouraged when they asked for my resume. I promised to send it right away.

When I had finally managed both living quarters and a job, it was time to tell Malek of my plans. I truly dreaded this moment. I felt ungrateful and deceitful. He took it in a stoic manner. He looked at me and said he saw that coming for quite some time.

"You are like the wind, Susan. No one can hold you. You came into my life and swept me away with you. But the wind does not stand still. It moves on to different places. I do hope you find what you are looking for. Good speed, young lady."

And so, my two years with Malek ended on a melancholy note. I moved to Frankfurt. This was far enough, or so I thought, from my father's grip. I moved in with my roommate, Irene, and got the supermarket job. The job payed barely enough to make ends meet, but I was happy with my new life. It paid the bills and that was all I needed.

Irene was a mysterious person. I wondered where she worked. She seemed to have a graveyard shift because she constantly left the house in the early evening and came back late at night. I noticed that she drank a lot, but I was not overly concerned. After all, that was her business. Between us we were able to pay the rent and that was all I cared about. Irene was a few years older than me. I was twenty-one by now and she was twenty-five. Life seemed steady and we had settled into a routine. Frankfurt was very different from my hometown. There were huge shopping centers and crowded streets. No one knew me here, which I considered a blessing. I did not run into my father and that gave me a kind of peace. I began to feel quite secure.

I had found serenity. While I barely made ends meet, I was happy. I began to relax. Then I made a mistake. I called my mother to see how she was doing. We had an amiable conversation, but she must have told my father about it. I had not sworn her to secrecy, so, I had no one to blame but myself. I had given her my phone number and now he knew it too.

It was a Tuesday morning when I saw my father standing at my apartment door. I had just returned from work. He must have looked the address up in the phone book. I was shocked beyond belief. At the first moment, I was paralyzed with fear.

"Well," he said to me in a patronizing tone, "aren't you ask me to come in?"

I finally found my voice and said, my heart racing with anxiety, "No I won't. I did not invite you here in the first place. You came here for nothing. Have a good day."

He looked at me with a face contorted with fury.

"Is this how you speak to me, you little ungrateful whore?"

At this moment my neighbor next door arrived at his apartment door. He saw the fear in my face and asked if this man was harassing me.

I answered, "No, he was just leaving. But thank you for your concern."

My father's rage was plain on his face, but he left.

Meanwhile, my peace of mind had vanished. How could I have been so stupid and call my mother? Of course he would find out. Now what was I going to do? My first instinct was to move again. Every fiber of my being was against it though.

Running again? I had just moved here. I had barely left Malek. I could not keep on doing that. And if I moved again, that would have to be my last time. Then came another thought. What was I even thinking? I had no money for a deposit or moving expenses. I simply could not afford it.

But now my father knew where to find me. My nightmares would return, as would my anxiety. I would be trapped again. I would be startled every time the phone rang. I would be back at square one. What was I going to do?

It was a Friday and I was off for the weekend. I decided to wait up for Irene. It turned out to be a long wait. I had nodded off a few times. She finally turned up at 2:30am. She was surprised to see that I was not in bed. She looked worn out and tired. She poured herself a cup of tea and asked what was the matter. I came straight to the point and asked her what her line of work was. She gave me a questionable look.

"What is this sudden interest in my affairs about?"

"I do not want to interfere in your privacy. I would just like to know," I said miffed.

"Of course, darling, no problem," Irene answered airily. "Then I will give you a straight answer. I am a prostitute."

This neither shocked nor surprised me. I had suspected as much. I was in no position to judge anyone. After all, I was contemplating doing the same thing. So, my next question came matter of fact.

"How much does it pay?'

Irene could not help but laugh. "There! That is the right attitude, my dear," she said. "Think of the money first and worry about the moral later, if at all."

She looked at me seriously and all humor was gone from her face when she addressed the question in more detail.

"Susan, you can make good money in this business, but it comes at a great price and is also very risky. Let me address the money first. If you work in a club and you make a thousand a night, the owner of the club will take half. Still on six days a week, $3,000 of pure money is within the realm of possibility. You could make ten thousand in a month. Of course, you will have some expenses. But the money is infinitely more than what you would make as a cashier in a supermarket."

Irene continued, "But... and make no mistake, there is a but. There are risks involved. The greatest risk of them all are the pimps. Those guys are like slave owners. If they have you in their grip, they take your money and never let you go. Or you could end up like me, not knowing how to get out of this business. Yes, don't think for a moment that this trade does not have a hold on you, even without pimps. You get addicted to that illusion of power this job seems to give you. The power over men. You will find out just how crazy some men are when it comes to sex. Once you have tasted that power it is hard to give it up. Of course, the money is part of it, too. Where else can you make that kind of money in such a short time if you do not have a college degree?"

Irene then looked at me with a hint of amusement.

"Are you considering joining the profession?" she asked with open curiosity.

I did not waiver and answered just as candidly, "Yes."

"Well, and there you have it," said Irene.

Suddenly, laughter shook her. It shook me, too. We slid off the couch, sat on the floor, and indulged in a laughing fit until our bellies hurt. We nearly choked with laughter and rang for air.

"Oh god," I blurted and dissolved into wild giggles again, "there is nothing funny about it."

After a while, we went to bed exhausted and exhilarated for no good reason. When we woke up it was nearly noon. We had a breakfast of toast and jelly with coffee. It was me who brought up the subject about my venture into prostitution again.

"Well," said Irene, "if you really want to go there, we need to go shopping first. You need teddies and high heels. Makeup as well."

"You mean, I wear nothing but a teddy and heels at the bar?" I asked shocked.

Irene nodded, "Yes, that would be your working outfit. Before we go into further detail, however, I want to know if you remember my sermon about this occupation before the laughing fit. I was quite serious before I lost it."

I nodded and said solemnly, "Yes, I remember."

"Now then, let's go shopping and then I'll introduce you to the owner of Club Athena."

When we got to the department store, we started at the shoe section. I chose high heeled black pumps with round toes. When Irene said I would need a second pair, I opted for the same style in silver. And for good measure I grabbed one additional pair in gold.

Next, we visited the negligee department. I chose teddies in black, silver, gold, and lavender. Irene watched me with interest.

"You are not into gaudy," she said dryly. "Even for the purpose those outfits are intended, I do believe in your case that might work well! It suits you somehow, this not screaming for attention."

"Irene," I said, "Understand this: I am only in this for the money. I will not do it for long either. It makes me uncomfortable and it is scary. I will tell you exactly why I am doing this. I am going to get a ticket to New York and after I have enough money, I will never do this again. I just need to get out of the country so I will get out of the clutches of my father. If I stay in Germany, I will never get out of his grip and I will be under his command forever. I just have to be careful that I will not get out of his grasp only to fall victim to another. The minute I suspect one of those pimps is on to me I will jump ship. I know plenty about being controlled already. The thought of being dominated by anyone again, leads me into sheer panic. I have got to make it without falling into that trap again.

"Okay, okay," Irene looked at me, "Good luck then and be careful."

After we finished shopping, we took a cab that took us to the Club Athena. The club owner's name was Herbie. He said he would charge five hundred a night for the use of his club.

"What if I have no customers?" I asked.

"You will," he said confidently. "But even if you don't, I will not charge you."

I was starting that very night to see if I was "cut out" for it. I had not yet quit my supermarket job in case this would not work out.

Soon it was 7:00pm and Irene and I boarded the train to head back for Club Athena. We changed into our job uniforms. I had chosen the black teddy and the black pumps for my first night on the job. Black was just right, I thought. I felt like I was going to my own funeral and burying the rest of my soul. I sat at the bar and felt like a calf going to slaughter. The doors had just opened and the first customers strolled in.

Two men sat down at the left end of the bar and eyed us with interest. We were two of the five girls on display, all in teddies all in high heels. I sat exactly in the middle and was observed closely. I was regarded as fresh meat, Irene told me. I found myself terrified and prayed that they would not be interested in me. No such luck, however. The older of the two men spoke to Herbie behind the bar. Shortly after their chat the club owner informed me that Mr. Brunner had requested my company. My heart beating painfully, I got up and moved over to the left side of the bar next to Mr. Brunner. He was approximately sixty years old and was balding with a bulging middle. He was kind of fatherly and nice toward me, which I could appreciate.

He ordered champagne and asked me my name. I had learned from Irene that I had to get a fake name. I chose Reyna. In a way, a false name was a great thing. I could pretend that the person who sat here for sale was not really me. Mr. Brunner made some small talk and then got straight to the point. He waived to Herbie and then told me he would book me for an hour. The fee was three hundred for that time. It would not bring me any profit because five hundred was mentioned as the fee for the use of the club. Well in any case, this was it. I grabbed the basket with the soap, the towel, and the condom and off we went to the showers. This was already quite nerve wrecking for me. After surviving the cleaning part, it was off to the privacy of a designated room. By this time, I was totally weirded out. This was so surreal.

Mr. Brunner was obviously nervous too. He ejaculated before I even dropped the towel. Much to my surprise, this shamed him to tears. I felt very sorry for him and consoled him as best as I could. I actually had deep compassion for the poor man. I told him that this was no tragedy and it could happen. That seemed to relax him. He said I was a nice girl and he would call on me again. Then he kissed me on the cheek and asked me if I would tell the other girls about his mishap. I assured him that his secret was safe with me. He hugged me, kissed me again, and got dressed. We went back to the bar. Mr. Brunner smiled at Herbie and me, and left the club.

It was only 8:00pm on my first night and I had had my first customer. Meanwhile the club had filled up considerably. The girls all had potential clients sitting next to them. As soon as I had sat down again at the end of the bar, I had another customer keeping me company. This one was a man of around fifty years old with a pleasant face and impeccably creased pants. My glance fell on the wedding ring that he wore on his left ring finger. My peek had not gone unnoticed by him.

"My wife does not understand me. All she cares about is getting her nails done, shopping for clothes, and buying jewelry. Meanwhile I am working my ass off and get depressed. I so want some peace," he explained.

I looked at him quizzically, "And you think you will find peace in this place?"

"Maybe not peace exactly, but at least some understanding. Here I pay 300 marks, I get myself taken care of, and I spare myself the humiliation to ask my wife for sex she does not want."

His answer did surprise me. This was pretty straightforward and it made sense in a way. I figured no matter what the different circumstances were, everyone was a product of their upbringing in some form. The way we were taught as a child has an impact all through life. The thought did not exactly cheer me up. Good luck then with your bullshit, I said to myself.

In the end, I took up his offer. I carried the basket again from the shower to the room. The sex was a pretty straight forward affair. I had now had two customers and earned six hundred marks, so I actually had made one hundred marks for myself. I was profiting and it was not yet 10:00.

At 10:30 I was chosen again. I was excited. This one meant all the money would go into my pocket. I was not so sure about this customer however. He seemed weird to me. Mid-forties and a very nervous attitude. Impeccably dressed in an Armani suit and complete with an expensive watch. He did not talk much; he just bought me a drink and said I could take it to the room. He paid the fee for 2 hours, which was 600 mark, all mine this time. I should have been excited, but I was actually terrified. What was I supposed to do in two hours?

We took the customary shower and then went into the designated room. I was about to shed the towel when he stopped me.

"You can leave that on. I won't touch you," he informed me.

What on earth was that all about, I thought uneasily. Oh god, please do not let this be something totally weird!

It turned out to be weird but in a good way. He took a fancy in watching me sleep. Well, I thought with a twinge of amusement, it takes all kinds and who am I to complain? This was easy money after all. I would take it and run with it.

This concluded my first day on the job as a prostitute. When Irene and I finally got back to our apartment, I found myself drained. I felt I was not really cut out for this, but my mantra was, that the end justified the means. I would be able to leave Germany and start a new life in the United States. If my first night on the job was any indication, it would not take that long. At least now I got money as a reward so I could use it to fulfill a dream. My dream was to live in the States and be free. Having this purpose firmly ingrained in my mind helped. I could now minimize the moral tumult by reasoning that escape from my father would be worth everything. I was doing an uncomfortable thing for a little while and in the end I would escape hell. Being a prostitute for a little while and doing it only to free myself, I could live with that.

In the end, I was in this business for only six weeks. It was not hard for me to quit because I never felt empowered by it. Unlike Irene, I never got attached to it. Neither the money nor the constant tension of falling into the hands of a pimp was incentive enough for me to make this profession a permanent line of work. It was interesting in some way to find out a few things about human desires. There are different tastes in clothes and movies and also in sexual activities. Sex was a wide field. While I was in the paid profession of sex, I was able to examine my own nature in that area. I was not against trying new things in general, but I had limits of my tolerance.

On one memorable occasion, a customer had taken a fancy to me and he was informing Herbie that he wanted to rent me for an hour. Herbie knew this man well, and said point blank that I was a bad choice for the activities he preferred.

"Look my man," said Herbie carefully, "Reyna is not a good fit you. She will laugh I just know it. She is relatively new and has not lost her sense of humor yet. I'm not sure her type ever will. Be smart and chose another girl for your venture."

"No," the customer replied stubbornly, "I want Reyna."

"Suit yourself," said Herbie. "But you won't get your money back if this doesn't work out. You have been warned."

After the shower ritual we went to the designated room. The customer instructed me to sit on the bed cross-legged with a robe on. Then he handed me what I first thought was a belt. After closer inspection I found out that it was a dog leash. This confused me greatly. Was I supposed to take part in a whipping session? It had been one of my conditions from day one that I would not do BDSM. The client had noticed my look and assured me I had nothing to fear, he was not going to whip me at all. He instructed me to put the collar and the leash on him. I did so with growing unease, horror, and amusement.

Then came the order that made any fight against wild giggles of laughter an impossibility. He asked me to order him to bark. My heroic fight against laughter was lost. It took everything I had, not to make a sound, but I lost that battle in the end. My belly hurt and my eyes streamed. I positively choked with merriment. When he began to run on all fours around the bed, barking like mad, I dissolved into new fits of laughter. While in between laughs I apologized for my behavior, I just could not help it. This was just too much. The client was not happy with me. He got dressed and marched out of the room to complain to Herbie. Herbie listened unsympathetically.

He placed his arms firmly on his hips and said, "I told you so. I know Reyna well enough to know that your type of routine will make her laugh. Not maliciously and not even at you, but on the art form itself. No way would she be able to control that. She hasn't acquired the necessary bitterness yet that would enable her to take that stoically."

I was six weeks into this job at Club Athena when a man entered the establishment. He wore black leather pants, a black dress shirt nearly unbuttoned to the navel, and several gold chains around his neck. When I saw him, all alarm bells went off simultaneously in my head. I recognized him as a pimp immediately.

I slid off the bar stool I was sitting on and excused myself to use the bathroom. I did not use the restroom but went to the locker room instead. I got dressed in a hurry, grabbed my purse, and did not even pick up the money that I earned that night. I went straight to the exit. At that very moment, a client arrived in a cab. As soon as the customer was out of the taxi, I went in. I knew immediately that my time was up when that character had taken a seat at the table, eyeing us girls on the bar. There were stakes I was okay with risking, but these were decisively too high. I was willing to cut my losses and run.

I headed for my apartment and packed my clothes in a hurry. I hastily scribbled a note to Irene, left a few bills on the table for my upcoming rent, and wished her luck. I had the cab waiting for me and asked the driver to take me to a hotel in the suburbs. I had enough money for a ticket to New York by now.

Time to move on. Freedom was so close I could taste it. A giddy excitement flushed through me. This time I would be gone for good.

Chapter 15

Free

"The most important kind of freedom is to be what you really are. You trade in your reality for a role. You trade in your sense for an act. You give up your ability to feel and in exchange put on a mask. There can't be any large-scale revolution, until there is a personal revolution, on an individual level. It's going to happen inside first" (Jim Morrison)

I left Frankfurt unscathed and was now at my grandmother's house. I did not tell her about my latest lifestyle.

Some things are better left alone, even if my grandmother was a tolerant and modern woman. The decision was easily made since she did not ask any questions.

I did tell her that I would be leaving for New York very soon. After some consideration, I decided I wanted to say goodbye to my mother. I asked my grandmother if she could call her. I was afraid to call myself for fear of my father picking up the phone. My grandmother agreed. My mother would come to see me before my departure.

Meanwhile I prepared for my move to New York. I read the local newspaper and applied for a job as an Au Pair girl. An appointment was set up for an interview with the brother of the advertiser, who lived in a nearby city. I was selected and was now ready to pack my suitcase. I had already booked my flight. It was arranged that I was to be picked up at Kennedy airport on the following Friday.

I could hardly believe it. It all happened so fast. I was going to be free! I was flying to the land of the free! The country I had admired for so long. An incredible feeling of happiness flooded through me. The wild elation was coupled with a slight fear. Was I scared? Of course I was. At least a little. I wondered if all of this would work out. I knew once I left Germany I wouldn't come back. Exactly how I was going to accomplish this was unclear. I would cross that bridge when I got there.

There was nothing left to do except say goodbye to my mother. She had agreed to come and not tell my father about my leaving the country. I guess this was one of the few times where she kept a secret from him. She took the short bus ride and arrived the day before my departure at my grandmother's house.

I saw her coming up the road that led to my grandmother's house. She had a bewildered expression on her face. As she climbed up the stairs to my grandmother's house, I saw the panic on her face. Finally, she stood before Ruth and me. She skipped the formalities and addressed her mother first.

"Mama, we cannot let her go," she said without preamble. "The whole thing is utterly impossible. You must help me change her mind."

My grandmother looked at her and there was pity and compassion on her face. She gave my mother an odd look and that look was not lost on Margaret.

"Margaret," she said gently, "we have long lost the right to tell Susan anything. I was never one who tells people what to do anyway. You should know."

My mom was astounded and taken a back, "Mama you are not going to help me talk some sense into Susan?"

Ruth sighed, "Margaret, we must let her go. I let you go when you got married. I am not going to dig into old wounds, but you did not listen to me. Susan will not listen to us either. I will be honest... I am not even sure she should listen to us.

Maybe she got it right, leaving the country. Who knows? In any case, it is her decision not ours."

Tears welled up in my mother's eyes. I felt it was time to say something.

"Mama, please try to understand. I am not leaving because I want to hurt you. I just need to find my own identity. I feel I am such a lost soul right now. I cannot find myself here. I have tried for more than twenty years. I cannot find myself, as long as your husband is in close proximity of me. You have decided to stay with him and that is your prerogative. It is your life and I am not telling you what to do. Please give me the same consideration. Let me go, Mama."

My mother looked at me with frightened eyes.

"You always wanted to leave. I have never understood you. You are my daughter but you are such a mystery to me. You are such an odd person. I am so worried about you. Don't go."

"Oh Mama, I have to. You are an enigma to me, too. I do not understand you anymore than you do me. As long as we love each other, it does not matter."

I hugged her then and said, "Good bye, Mama."

I walked her to the bus stop and it was my turn to tear up. When she stepped onto the bus a feeling of deep sorrow welled up in me. The bus would take her back to her house of horrors. A feeling of melancholy swept over me that I found hard to shake.

The next morning was misty and cool. I stood in front of my grandmother's house with my suitcase beside me. My uncle had the car pulled up; he would take me to the train station. The airport was in Duesseldorf. That was approximately a two-and-a-half-hour train ride. From there I would board the plane to New York.

I hugged my grandmother one last time and was surprised when she asked for my forgiveness. I saw tears in her eyes, which surprised me even more. She never cried.

"You want me to forgive you? For what?" I asked with genuine surprise. "You never let me down."

She looked at me with a serious expression on her face.

"Yes, I have," she said. "And your mother as well. I closed my mind when you asked for help. May god forgive me and hopefully you too, Susan."

I kissed her on the cheek.

"I have always forgiven you for that. The fact is, I have never blamed you for it. I have blamed Mama, though. I will have to find a way to forgive her. In my heart, I know she is not to blame. I am going to work on it. In time, I will have to forgive my father as well. I am not ready yet, though."

I hugged her one more time and climbed into the car. I waved until I could not see her anymore. We arrived at the train station. I thanked my uncle for the ride and said goodbye. The train left and my hometown disappeared in the distance. I did not look back. When we reached Duesseldorf, I grabbed a cab and drove to the airport.

When the plane was ready to board, I settled into my seat and fastened my seatbelt. I reflected on my young life. I was twenty-two years old. I had yet to find my identity. I did not know what the future would bring. I was ready to start fresh. I was full of hope. Hope is always a good starting point. I took a deep breath as the plane taxied on the runway. As we gathered speed and the plane took off, I closed my eyes and felt free.

Sequel

... And Then Came Grace

To be continued...

My new life in New York was full of challenges as well. I faced a many obstacles which included the perhaps greatest battle of my life: my personal combat with immigration.

I shall be delighted my dear readers if you join me into the second part of my life.

Thank you!

Works Cited

George, Katherine. "Narcissistic Personality Disorder: Diagnosis, Causes, Treatments." *WebMD*, WebMD, 18 June 2020,

www.webmd.com/mental-health/narcissistic-personality-disorder#1.

Meyers, Seth. "Narcissistic Parents' Psychological Effect on Their Children." *Psychology Today*, Sussex Publishers, 1 May 2014, www.psychologytoday.com/us/blog/insight-is-2020/201405/narcissistic-parents-psychological-effect-their-children.